WHAT OTHERS ARE SAYING ...

"This is a fantastic read with lots of [...]
wish I had read something like this [...]
management journey, as it would have helped a huge
amount! A great job, Emma Sharrock, and I could not more
highly recommend this to aspiring project managers or even
existing ones, who may learn something new!"

Stephen Dowling, ETM Management Training (CEO & Founder)

"Emma is one of the most capable project managers I have
worked with. She's organised, unflappable and sets the
standard for Agile delivery. Outside of work, Emma's
dedication to achieving personal goals, from completing
triathlons to writing this book, is inspiring. I learned an
extraordinary amount from working alongside her, and would
encourage anyone who is interested in change or project
management to read this book and learn from one of the
best."

Ellen Cresswell, Digital Professional

"Emma's beautiful writing will have you engaged in the world
of managing projects the Agile way from the first page of this
book. Throughout the entire book, Emma will have you
thinking about your current personal and professional projects,
making it a worthwhile read for anyone. Her personal stories,
knowledge and wisdom will definitely help you become a
better project manager, but will also give you great tools to
help you navigate and succeed in today's constantly
changing world."

Eduardo Nofuentes, The Agile Contact Centre

"If you picked this book up thinking it may be a technical project management guide, you'd be wrong! It's so much more than that. Incorporating ideas from the Agile methodology, it demystifies change and simplifies what we often overcomplicate when managing change projects. Breaking down the key areas where projects typically go wrong, *The Agile Project Manager* provides effective ways to manage the often tricky people aspects of projects. Not sure how to get people on board? Facing resistance from key stakeholders? Grappling with scope creep, big risks and issues? Stop worrying and pick up this book!

Widely referenced and drawing on examples from her own life, the author shares how to apply the ideas, techniques and tools to successfully achieve goals at work and in life.

Emma's conversational style makes this book easy to read and digest. It's as if she's sitting alongside you, guiding you every step of the way. Using analogies, metaphors and real-life stories from her vast project management and coaching experience, she becomes your own personal coach.

Asking you questions you may not have thought to ask yourself, *The Agile Project Manager* is an inspiring and practical guide for anyone who aspires to deliver successful projects and make change happen. It could be the project manager's new best friend."

Caroline Cameron, Executive Coach, Possibility to Reality

"Emma Sharrock has written the book that all IT professionals need to read. We all work in IT, but first we are all human beings. Change is a constant for us in work and in life, and Emma's approach helps us all learn how to help ourselves. A must-read."

Catherine Lockstone, Consulting Executive

"When so much has already been said about a subject, it takes something very different to make you think, something that I was fortunate enough to do with *The Lazy Project Manager*. In this book *The Agile Project Manager*, Emma has approached the world of project management from a very personal perspective, and by projects this encompasses business change as well as personal change. The result is a book that I found very readable and therefore enjoyable, and a book that offers up a raft of practical means to address the very typical challenges any would-be Agile project manager will face."

Peter Taylor, *The Lazy Project Manager*

"Many have attempted to formulate and articulate what Agile is. What Emma shares is her astute experience on what the key Agile principles are and how they apply to achieve success in ANY change – she has pulled it off! Everyone interested in Agile – in being an excellent project manager – needs to read this book."

Lisa Poulton, Coach @ Maximise Talent

Published in Australia by
Agile Enterprises
Postal: GPO Box 1481, Canberra ACT 2601
Tel: +61 404 624 314
Email: info@theAgileprojectmanager.com
Website: www.theagileprojectmanager.com.au

First published in Australia 2015
Copyright © Emma Sharrock 2015

National Library of Australia Cataloguing-in- Publication entry

Sharrock, Emma
THE AGILE PROJECT MANAGER: Thrive in change with Agile

ISBN: 978-0-9944621-0-7
Project Management - software
Project Management - computer programs
Dewey Number: 658.4040285

Editing: Mary-Jo O'Rourke AE
Illustrations: Finch Creative
Cover design: *popdesign*
Author photography: Ramona Lever

Disclaimer
All care has been taken in the preparation of the information herein, but no responsibility can be accepted by the publisher or author for any damages resulting from the misinterpretation of this work. All contact details given in this book were current at the time of publication, but are subject to change.

The advice given in this book is based on the experience of the individuals. Professionals should be consulted for individual problems. The author and publisher shall not be responsible for any person with regard to any loss or damage caused directly or indirectly by the information in this book.

THE AGILE PROJECT MANAGER

Thrive in change with Agile

Emma Sharrock

ABOUT THE AUTHOR

An experienced project manager, Agile enthusiast and coach, Emma is passionate about all things that involve change and people. She has been delivering projects for over fifteen years, and founded a coaching business in 2011. Since then she has been seeking ways to 'converge' her passions for projects and change, and human behaviour.

Emma feels strongly that in this increasingly complex world, we are losing the human aspect of project and change management. We are prioritising tools and templates over relationships and human interaction. It is getting harder to take the time to meet with someone face to face to understand their concerns when there are a million spreadsheets waiting to be completed and new processes that need to be followed.

Her goal with *The Agile Project Manager* is to provide simple tools and techniques that assist project professionals to achieve project success. These tools and techniques are all about you, the reader, because that is where the greatest difference can be made.

DEDICATION

To my wonderful husband, Damo, my biggest fan, strongest supporter and love of my life.

ACKNOWLEDGMENTS

When writing a book about the mindset and principles of honesty, transparency and collaboration, it is impossible to do without the help of a team of people. A team of people who are happy to give honest feedback on progress, as well as encouragement along the way.

Rob Thomsett, my mentor, whom I had the privilege of working with for three years at NAB. He has been my inspiration, my Yoda and the reason this book first came into being. His patient feedback on my ideas, as well as the opportunity to see him in action and learn from him firsthand, are things I am so grateful for.

Alice Haemmerle, my coach and mentor, whom I have learned so much from. Her insights into life and her support and encouragement, not to mention the incredible community she has built by attracting only the best people, have been central to my successes.

My editor, Mary-Jo, who has provided direct feedback on my writing style, including quote corrections I would have missed and great ideas for illustrations. I love our catch-ups over wine to talk all things from editing the book to solving the problems of the world. I'm looking forward to collaborating with you on more books.

My illustrator, Kathryn, who has brought to life the little character you see throughout the book. She easily translated my sketchy design briefs into real-life art. It's a talent I wish I had.

My *Agile Project Manager* team early adopters:

Priya – my long-time friend who gave me tons of encouragement at a well-needed time.

Darrell – who signed up immediately and was always up for some sage advice at the right time.

Maddy – a fabulous sounding board and cheer squad, her enthusiasm was infectious and her feedback was incredibly helpful.

Greg – my fellow coach at NAB: I am so grateful for your advice and help along the way, as I'm sure you are grateful for my help with your Twitter presence.

Adrian and his wife Denise – they signed up immediately and avidly retweeted my blog posts, which I so appreciated.

Blair – a fantastic first fast follower, always retweeting and prompting me for updates.

Ellen – my amazing boss for a short time at Coles, with her impeccable writing style and great feedback on my writing and content, including helping me get over my love of exclamation marks.

My *Agile Project Manager* team reviewers:

Lani Beer

Parth Bommakanti

Caroline Cameron

Clare Cope

Stephen Dowling

Emma Gangemi

Chris Griggs

John Jeston

Venkatesh Krishnamurthy

Catherine Lockstone

Eduardo Nofuentes

Lisa Poulton

Peter Taylor

You will never know how helpful you have been. On the days when the words refused to come out onto the page, to receive a tweet, a text, an email or a phone call asking how the book was going or providing feedback on something I'd sent out was such a boost and always welcome, no matter where I was in the writing journey. There were great days, there were average days, and you were always there.

CONTENTS

Foreword

I remember very clearly when I first met Emma.

I was building an Agile project management framework for a major Australian bank and, as part of my contract, I had agreed to create, coach and mentor a small team of Agile project management coaches to embed and sustain the tools, techniques and cultural change that supported a very different approach to traditional project governance and project management.

Having developed and implemented components of my approach to Agile project management in US, UK and Australian organisations, I knew the person I was looking for and how hard it would be to find such a person. In particular, I was looking for a person who had learned what I have always believed is a fundamental truth about projects and change:

Project management is all about people and relationships.

All the great project managers I had met had learned this truth and were experts at communication, and building and maintaining great relationships with their teams, their stakeholders and, most importantly their sponsors. They were both empathetic and focused and, more importantly, open to change and learning. They knew their strengths and weaknesses.

So, I was waiting in the foyer of the bank. I didn't know what Emma looked like and assumed that somehow we'd find each other. There were many people milling around, talking in small groups and, like me, waiting to meet someone.

Suddenly this person walked up to me, put her hand out and said, "You must be Rob. I'm Emma and I'm really pleased to meet you."

At that very moment, I knew Emma was the person we needed. She joined the bank and for nearly two years I watched as she coached, supported, taught and listened to project managers as they went through the difficult transition from traditional to Agile project management. Emma learned too throughout those years, both from her work in the bank and from her private consulting work. Those learnings are throughout this book.

You see, the courage, self-awareness and openness that Emma had shown in coming up to me and engaging me in a conversation are the keys to becoming a great Agile project manager. In addition, a passion for exploring different sources of knowledge and learning from them is the secret to remaining a truly Agile project manager.

To me, a great day is a day when we learn something.

I have learned from Emma and when you read this book, you will have many great days.

Rob Thomsett
Canberra 2015

Introduction

The world around us is constantly changing. And changing faster than ever. Are you ready?

If your answer is no, don't worry, as not many of us are ready. Our mindsets are still effectively geared for the Industrial Revolution and yet here we find ourselves in the Information Age. We need to adapt quickly, not just to survive, but also to thrive. Whether we like it or not, we are all in the business of change.

This book is about this business of change. You may well be the subject of the title – a project manager or a change manager. You may just as well be a teacher, a lawyer, a doctor, a parent, a party planner or someone organising to move house. This book is written for all of you.

My goal for you is that reading this book will help you not only to thrive in this everchanging world, but also to achieve your purpose and aspirations, so that change happens on YOUR terms.

I am passionate about helping people to achieve amazing results by highlighting that these results are simpler to achieve than you may think. I've worked in project and change management for over fifteen years and now, as a coach, there are certain themes that I adhere to throughout my work which help to make change easy and effortless. When applied, these insights can help turn a potential disaster into an unqualified success.

One theme that informs my day-to-day coaching above all is the importance of being 'Agile'. The Agile concept has formally been around since 2001 when the *Manifesto for Agile Software Development* was published; however, Agile concepts have been practised informally since the 1980s. The

Agile approach first endeavoured to make the complex process surrounding software development simple. But why apply this approach only to software delivery when the underlying concepts could be applied to anything?

Everyone deserves to achieve amazing results, and through my coaching I've learned to understand that with the right mindset and the right supporting tools, achieving those amazing results can be a lot easier than you think.

American author and motivational speaker Zig Ziglar once said that we are all in the business of sales. Whether it is our formal profession or not, we must all sell ourselves and sell what we do. I take that further and say we are all in the business of change. And with our lives changing so rapidly, we need to be excellent agents of change, large and small. Big change requires planning, scheduling and a steady approach. Smaller changes require fast decisions and quick action. I call this the project continuum. It doesn't matter where you are located on the continuum: the more Agile your approach, the greater success you will have.

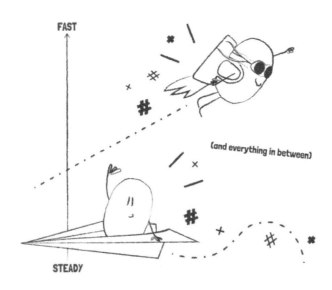

We all manage change all of the time, so whether it is our job title or not, we are ALL project managers. The TV series *The Apprentice* (a reality TV show originally aired in the USA where contestants compete against each other to win the prize of becoming the 'apprentice' to a successful celebrity business personality – in the USA it was Donald Trump, in the UK Sir Alan Sugar and in Australia Mark Bouris) did wonders in advertising the project manager role to the mass market and showing that anyone (with varying degrees of success) can do it. So, if we are all doing it all of the time, why not do it really, really well?

What is a Project?

Since we are all project managers, we need to agree on what a project is. According to *The Project Management Body of Knowledge (PMBOK Fifth Edition)*:

> "A project is a temporary endeavor
> to create a unique product service or result."

The key word here is 'unique'. Anything that you do over and over again, from cleaning your teeth or mowing the lawn to paying bills, is NOT a project. Even moving house, if done often enough (heaven forbid), could be considered a process; however, for most of us this doesn't happen too often and even if it does, it is most likely unique every time.

Here is a handy tool that Stephen Dowling from ETM Management Training uses to show the extreme differences between projects and 'business as usual' activities.

What's the difference?

Area	Project Activity	Operations Activity
Life Cycle of the activity?	Start and a finish	No definitive beginning and end
Products, service or result produced?	Unique, once off	Repeated
People or resources used?	Specific for project	Normal operations
Costs to complete?	Specific for project	On-going costs
Risks in doing the activity?	New risks	Existing risks
Organisational change as a result of doing?	Will bring change	No significant change

How different are these?   What happens if you stuff them up?

The great thing about defining a project this way is that we can all identify with the concept. In this constantly changing world, we must undertake unique actions all the time to simply keep up with what is going on. And projects can be done extremely well or extremely badly. Let's make the decision right now to do them well using some simple techniques and practices.

So What Does Agile Mean?

This means many things to many people and so it's important to define the Agile concept here to make sure we're all on the same page. One dictionary definition states that it is "the ability to move quickly and easily". The *Manifesto for Agile Software Development* states:

"We are uncovering better ways of developing software

by doing it and helping others do it.

Through this work we have come to value:

18

Individuals and interactions over processes and tools

Working software over comprehensive documentation

Customer collaboration over contract negotiation

Responding to change over following a plan

That is, while there is value in the items on the right,

we value the items on the left more."

This statement was signed by the 22 founders of Agile software development and since then Agile development has grown into a variety of methodologies and given birth to an industry of its own. It has had great success in some organisations and limited success in others.

With this in mind, the Agile project manager is a person just like you who can take control in an everchanging world in order to make change effortless. The Agile PM does this through a mindset that embraces some basic principles that result in successful change every time.

The Agile Project Manager – a definition

You may have a burning question at this point: Are project managers even needed in projects using Agile techniques? If everyone is happily collaborating with each other and the customer, and delivering value in a flexible way, do they need someone to 'manage' it? This question gets asked a lot. Some people adamantly state that there is no need and others believe they are absolutely needed. The fact is: both views are right. There may well be projects (especially small ones with few dependencies) that need minimal project management oversight (as a formal role), whereas other projects will benefit from a project manager working with the team to support them. The principles detailed in this book are designed to assist with any change regardless of who embraces them and in what context.

With that in mind, the Agile PM is a smart, savvy individual who is equipped to manage change in the most effortless way possible and so as to thrive in a rapidly changing world.

Does that sound like you?

What This Book is About

This book is about why these basic Agile principles are so important and how they can be applied to achieve success in ANY change – from large-scale organisational change to something new in your personal life right now. This book is for YOU and how you can easily apply some simple principles to dramatically change the quality of your results and ultimately your life.

If you already know a bit about Agile, that's great – you can let me know if I get something wrong. If you don't know much about it, that doesn't matter, as you bring your own unique perspective.

What This Book is *not* About

This book does not go into the details of Agile software development. It does not discuss Scrum, Lean, Kanban or any other software-specific tool or technique. There are already some great books out there that talk about this.

Why You should Read This

Are you going through a change in your life, whether it is at work or at home? Are you prepared to make some small changes in your approach in order to achieve great results? I trust that by this point, you have decided it's worth investing in this book. I won't let you down!

My Story

My childhood was spent as a 'RAAF brat' because my parents were both in the Royal Australian Air Force. We moved around the country a number of times and change became a way of life. When my father retired at the start of my high school years, I approached the prospect of spending the rest of my school life at the same school with a mixture of relief and sadness. There was a part of me that loved the challenge of finding new friends and getting used to a new routine. There was another part that longed for permanence.

I left school and joined the Royal Australian Navy as an Officer of the Watch. A life of travel and adventure awaited! I completed a science degree at the Australian Defence Force Academy (ADFA) and first stumbled on the concept of organisational change while completing my honours year. I discovered, through my thesis research, that (wait for it) the more involved people feel in a change, the more likely they are to accept it (I know, it's big). My passion for people and for change was ignited and everything I chose to do from that moment fed the fire.

Since then, I have become an avid reader of anything to do with change and human behaviour, and this hasn't stopped. While in the Navy, I was given some projects to run. I never considered myself a project manager, but after doing it for a year I was offered the role in a consultancy. For the next few years, I found myself running project after project in the capacity of a project or change manager and LOVING it. I found myself continually fascinated by how people respond to change. For example, a large change involving job cuts and system changes could go very smoothly, while a small change preventing people from changing the colour of their background screen on their computer could result in hostility bordering on outright rebellion.

And this got me thinking ... The difference, the 'secret sauce', was not how big the change was, but rather the level of involvement of the people affected by the change – whether great or small.

From then on, I have been determined to help people to execute change in the simplest way, with the least effort and the best results. Enter the Agile approach.

Admittedly, when I first used Agile I was running a software project, but I quickly saw how these concepts could be applied to the parts of my project that were not Agile, and then further afield to other non-Agile projects. To areas of my personal life. To anything.

Eager to learn more, I became a Scrum Master for both the certification and the opportunity to learn Agile tools in more detail, as well as achieving a Diploma in Life Coaching. This opened the door to helping people on a deeper level, and the tools and techniques I learned and applied with my clients complemented the Agile tools perfectly. Everything started to come together and I realised that utilising simple Agile techniques and coupling them with an understanding of human behaviour are key to creating change that works.

Key Agile Concepts

Projects that follow Agile principles have these characteristics in common. They:

- are iterative
- show value along the way (not just at the end) – often using regular 'showcases'
- involve smart people who add value
- are open and transparent about progress
- have a team that is trustworthy and self-organising
- have a clear outcome or vision

- demonstrate flexibility in order to change what isn't working
- have regular catch-ups to evaluate progress – these are often called 'stand ups' and 'retrospectives'

Other Definitions

I use the terms 'resourceful' and 'unresourceful' throughout this book – especially in regards to behaviour – and they are worth understanding up front. *Resourceful* behaviours or actions are things people do that are good for them and for others. They help to move something forward. *Unresourceful* behaviour is the opposite. While it might be well intentioned, it does not contribute to anything helpful and could even result in things becoming worse.

You will also see the word 'ecological' – this is not just a reference to our natural world, but to everything in our environment. When you think about an action you plan to take, what are some of the impacts beyond yourself and your immediate environment? Setting a goal that moves you in a great direction but may potentially harm others is not an ecological goal.

You may also notice a few words specific to Agile such as 'Scrum' and 'backlog'. I make a number of references to the Agile values and principles. They are explained throughout and I have included a glossary at the back.

How This Book Works

One of the key principles of the Agile approach is doing things in small chunks, getting feedback and then adjusting where required. So that's how this book has been written. Every two to three weeks, a chapter was released via download to my subscribers as a 'showcase'. These amazing volunteers took the opportunity to read and digest the content, then provide feedback – the 'retrospective'.

The format of a retrospective is:

- What's worked well
- What hasn't worked well
- What still confuses me
- What we can do differently next time

Some of this was delivered face to face; other feedback was via phone and email. When giving feedback, there is no right or wrong. The purpose of the book retrospectives was to identify challenges early so the project (i.e. the book) could remain on track and on message. Everyone was encouraged to be open and honest and I remained open to all feedback. Everyone who participated receives acknowledgment, a gift and my eternal gratitude.

Reading This Book

As you read this book, as well as reading with your own purpose in mind, I encourage you to read through three different lenses (we're project managers after all, we can multi-task!):

1. Learning as a project or change manager and how this can help your project or change initiative

2. Learning as an individual and how this can help you personally

3. Learning with the objective of teaching these concepts to others

The chapters touch on lenses 1 and 2 interchangeably and you will take different things from each chapter depending on where you are right now in your personal and professional change journeys. Lens number 3 may not be something you were thinking about, but it is critical to achieving your outcome for this book. This is because when you learn something, the best way to remember it (and to use it effectively in your life) is to use the newly learned concept or tool AND to teach it to someone else.

Think about when you have learned something new, whether through reading an article or a book or even hearing it from someone. A couple of weeks later, you might struggle to recall the content or even WHEN you learned this nugget of gold – it may be forgotten altogether. However, if you tell someone else about it, you now have two reference points for your memory: the time you actually learned it AND the time you relayed this information to someone else. Your brain is very grateful for this additional boost. Plus you have helped someone else by teaching THEM something new. Do you see how this is win/win?

So, whenever anything resonates and you want to remember it, sure, write it down if you like (which will help too, by giving you another reference point), but also teach it to someone. Share the knowledge. Share the love.

Your brain will thank you for it, as will the person you share the information with. In fact, this very action may form part of your purpose for reading this book – to learn and share knowledge.

Key Concepts Covered

Chapter 1 – Know Your Why: this chapter focuses on the importance of having a purpose, so that when things get difficult, you keep moving forward. This is important for any type of change – personal or work-related. Without knowing the intention behind what you are doing, it is easy to lose focus and grind to a halt.

Chapter 2 – Know Your Risks: once you have defined your purpose and know where you are going, it's a good idea to brainstorm what could go wrong – not just things that could destroy your initiative, but things that could make the project more difficult than it should be. Spending a bit of time in this space is important so that you know what to do when things don't run to plan.

Chapter 3 – Know Your Team: no one is an island and rarely do great things happen without support from others. Who is on your team? From your stakeholders in a large project to your family and friends, take time to enlist some help.

Chapter 4 – Know Your Scope (or What's the What?): what do you need to do in order to achieve your purpose? What are the logical steps that must be taken? And what are things that, while they might be good to do, are not critical to achieving your purpose? Spending more time on high-value activities will fast-track your progress to achieving great results in anything.

Chapter 5 – Your Systems and Tools (the How): build the dream and understand success before understanding which tools or systems will help you to achieve it. There's no point in booking a removal truck if you don't know where you are moving to or what you are taking.

Chapter 6 – Opportunities for Excellence: be open to new possibilities that will help you to do things even better. This helps you to become ready to benefit fully from the work you are putting into achieving your desired purpose.

Chapter 7 – Stay True to your Vision: check your desired purpose regularly and ensure you stay true to what you have set out to do. This also helps you to reassess your vision – is this still what you want to do or have things changed?

Conclusion: a summary of key learnings and a personal action plan for you.

Remember, this is not only a book about project management and not only a book about personal change management techniques. It's about BOTH and how projects in the business world are related to change in our own lives. I absolutely believe that writing a book about Agile change management could not have been successful without open, transparent collaboration with people I trust. So the first chapters involved lots of feedback from people I know personally and trust professionally. Once the dream was built, I opened it up to the world …

I encourage you, as you read this book, to think about your dream. What do you want to achieve? What is your purpose? How can you use the principles we discuss here to build that dream and make it real? My hope for you in this book is that it doesn't just give you simple strategies to thrive in this everchanging world, but helps you to build your dream so that change happens on YOUR terms.

To your dream.

"A vision is not just a picture of what could be; it is an appeal to our better selves, a call to become something more."

Rosabeth Moss Kanter, Harvard Business School

What brings you to this book? What is your purpose for reading it? What are you looking to get out of it? Why read it at all? These are questions we don't often ask ourselves before we start something, whether a project, a house move or a relationship. When we understand why we are doing something, we are more likely to keep going when things get tough. Lose the Why and we lose the purpose. That is why it is so important that you have a purpose in reading this book. In reading ANY book. Without a purpose, you'll probably lose interest by Chapter 3 and start reading something else or go watch the latest episode of *Revenge* instead.

German philosopher Frederick Nietzsche once said, "He who has a why can bear any how". Knowing your Why is the first step to defining what success means to you. Every project is unique and every person is unique. So every definition of success is unique.

I encourage you to set your intention for this book right now by finishing this sentence: 'In order to make this book the most extraordinary book I have ever read, that has had the MOST impact on my life, I will achieve _____ as a result of reading it'.

Have you written anything down yet? Don't miss this step! It doesn't mean this book HAS to be the most extraordinary you have ever read. But if it WAS going to be the most extraordinary, what would that look like for you? What would make it great? Because even though the writing is all mine, the reading is all yours. What do you need to achieve to get the most out of the time you spend reading?

Time is our only finite resource and I am so grateful that you have chosen to invest some time in reading this book. Let's make sure you spend it in the best way for you. So go on, what do you want to achieve?

If you're finding it tough to articulate your purpose for reading this book, you're not alone. At some point in our lives, we all stopped asking Why? and just got on with things. This chapter is all about re-learning how to do something we are born to do, which is great news. It means this will be easy.

Why did We Stop Asking Why?

The fact that we don't ask Why? as much anymore is the fault of our parents. Really, it is. As children we are born naturally curious, born with wonder and awe at the world. We are always asking questions as we absorb the newness of the world around us. Our patient parents answer our constant questions:

'Why is the sky blue?'

'Why do cats have four legs?'

'Why does Daddy have to go to work?'

The list goes on. However, even the most saint-like parent will reach the point of exhaustion (children are pretty energetic creatures!) and say:

'Just because.'

'Because they just do.'

'Because I said so.'

While I say it's their fault, I'm not assigning blame. Sometimes our poor parents just needed a break. Unfortunately, what this does, over time, is discourage us from asking Why? We then move into school and university, get busy jobs, where asking questions can be interpreted as time-wasting. We start to make assumptions or become afraid to ask because somewhere in our minds, we fear that we should already know the answer and we don't want to look stupid.

I believe we are conditioned to keep our mouths shut and ask very few questions. Through the process of growing up, going to school and having to get from place to place efficiently, we lose our child-like wonder and curiosity about the world. We achieve our aim of not bothering people (i.e. our parents and teachers) as much, but at the same time we lose our ability to dream. We lose the capacity and ability to ask Why?

Before we breathe a collective sigh of relief (I KNEW it wasn't my fault!), it's time to take stock. The reason you stopped asking Why? may well have been because of your parents. The reason for you not asking Why? NOW is a personal choice. Your choice. It's time to take responsibility and do something different. To start asking Why?

Although I love the well-known quote from Mark Twain: "It is better to keep your mouth closed and let people think you are a fool than to open it and remove all doubt", this is a double-edged sword. There are definitely times in our lives when we are better off being quiet – when someone starts talking politics at a dinner party or when an ill-informed troll pipes up on social media (tempting, but in these cases remaining silent is best).

There are also times in our lives when we should not be quiet. In fact, there are times when we simply MUST speak up. Like when we're in a workshop and someone refers to an abbreviation, a system or concept, or something else we don't understand. And we need to understand it as part of our project or role.

A couple of years ago, I did a course alongside a wonderful woman called Yasmin. I didn't know her before this course and one of the first things that struck me was how many questions she asked. Whenever we covered something new, she would seek clarification by asking a question or proposing a scenario where this concept might be appropriate. My inner voice was saying 'wow, that's a lot of questions – she must not understand what we are talking about'.

But then she asked a question that I was thinking in my head. I was genuinely wondering, but had no intention of asking ('perhaps I'll work it out later when I do some further reading',

I may have told myself), and when Yasmin asked, I realised she was not seeking clarification or solving problems only for herself, but for the entire room. By being unafraid to speak up and ask, she was helping the whole room, which was full of people just like me who were sitting in silence and not asking what needed to be asked.

Then something interesting started to happen. More people started asking questions and seeking clarification. People (including me) seemed to realise that it was also up to us (not only the trainer) to learn what we needed to learn as the course continued. That course is still one of the best courses I have ever done, not just because of the amazing content and experience the trainer provided, but also because of the example Yasmin provided. The standard she set for learning.

It reminded me of the importance of asking Why? and truly seeking to understand something, rather than sitting quietly, taking notes and trusting that it will all come together later. Sometimes it does. Sometimes it doesn't. The big lesson I took from this training changed the way I approached the remainder of the training (and future trainings). I started to take responsibility for my own learning and ask the questions that needed to be asked, when they needed to be asked.

I started to ask Why?

Our ability to wonder and dream underpins everything we do. Our ability to know where we are going, our purpose, is critical. Imagine hopping into a taxi and asking the driver to take you 'anywhere but here'! A lovely, understanding driver might just drive you around until you calmed down. Another taxi driver might get impatient and not want to take you anywhere until you gave them a destination. In fact, some taxi drivers don't even let you into their cabs until you have a destination. This is a great metaphor for life – if you don't know your own purpose or destination, you're likely to end up at someone else's. Or stay exactly where you are.

> "If you don't know where you are going,
> any road will take you there."
>
> Lewis Carroll

Your Why is your purpose. It's your reason for living, for breathing, for doing anything. If you don't know it, any activity is going to occupy you but will leave you feeling empty.

Before you do anything, wonder why you are doing it. What purpose does it fulfil? Is it in line with your higher goals? Your higher self? This is especially important because some of the things we choose to do are hard and time-consuming. So much so, it's tempting to give up. With a big enough purpose, a big enough Why, you can keep going through tough times.

My big Why for this book is to share my passion and knowledge in Agile and personal change concepts, and how they can be used to achieve great project and personal results. Also, my friends and colleagues who knew about my passion and book idea were always asking me how it was going, because they wanted to read it. That was enough to keep me going through days of writer's block and the temptation to watch the new season of *The Mentalist*.

Simon Sinek, an author best known for his work in inspirational leadership, in his book *Start with Why* attributes Apple's success to its ability to sell you *why* it does what it does, not *what* it does. He calls this the Golden Circle – depicted below.

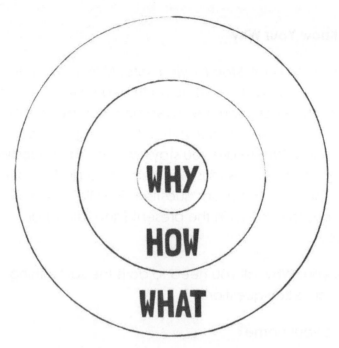

Ref: *Start with Why* Simon Sinek, 2013

When we understand the Why, then the How and the What are easier to figure out. And people are more interested in Why and could easily switch off if you go straight to the What or the How. Of course, there is always work to do after Why is established, but it is more focused and sustainable work. It is more believable and achievable, as it is directed towards a purpose. I trust I have convinced you that knowing why you do anything and everything that you do is critical to your success.

Knowing our own purpose is critical to the success of any change we are involved in. Whether we are the project manager or a team member in a change initiative at work, knowing our Why means that our contribution to our project's Why will be true and consistent with us and our own values.

How to Know Your Why

In her amazing book *Stop Playing Safe*, Margie Warrell observes how interesting it is going through airport security and customs, where you are asked on a number of occasions 'What is the purpose of your visit?', 'How long are you staying?' and 'Where are you staying?' So many questions! Yet so important, as it is those questions that protect our borders. They are important questions to reflect upon, as the implications to our lives in the present (and future) are immense.

To know your Why, all you need to do is the same thing. Ask yourself some key questions:

1. What is your name?

2. What is it that you do? What makes you come alive?

3. Who do you do it for? Who are the people who benefit most from what you do?

4. What do these people want and need? What are their deepest desires?

5. What are the tangible outcomes and results you give them? What is the evidence of this?

Being curious is the most important thing, because when you know your purpose, the thing that's going to make you leap out of bed every morning, well, you will leap out of bed every morning. How good is that?

Self-efficacy

Psychologist Albert Bandura has defined self-efficacy as "one's belief in one's ability to succeed in specific situations". Self-efficacy is different from self-esteem, as it is specific to certain situations and the confidence you have in yourself to succeed at that specific thing. For example, you may be excellent at running marathons but terrified at the prospect of sky-diving.

The good news is that self-efficacy can be increased over time by exposing yourself to unfamiliar situations and succeeding in them. By stepping outside your comfort zone and into your growth zone. This is uncomfortable (terrifying at times!), but if you summon the courage to step into it, you WILL grow. Your comfort zone will then grow in turn. Things that may have been uncomfortable in the past will become part of your day-to-day. Things that seemed impossible in the past will feel within reach.

My friend Lisa recently recovered from an injury and took up running. She would run for a minute, then walk, and slowly built up to running her first 5 km race. She was exhilarated to finish and immediately planned a 10 km run. Meanwhile, her friends were running half-marathons and she looked at those achievements with awe: "I just can't imagine running for 21 km! I don't think I can do it. I can't even picture it!"

Lisa got stronger and stronger and decided to enter a 15 km race, then a half-marathon. Within a year of taking her first tentative run/walk steps, she had completed a half-marathon. If she had entered a half-marathon within days of starting to learn to run, she probably would not have made it. What Lisa did was step out of her comfort zone and as she grew, so did her growth zone. And by building her self-efficacy in running, this gave her confidence in other areas of her life too.

What This Means for Your Projects

Now we have talked about you, let's take this into a professional context. What does this mean for a project or change initiative? Any project, large or small, simply MUST have a shared purpose. Have you ever been involved in a project where the critical stakeholders have not been aligned in their thinking? Or in conflict? Possibly even resulting in arguments in project meetings? Or worse ... NO arguments, just confused silence?

Projects can get messy. They can get complicated. People become tired. Without a shared purpose, a shared vision that the whole team can get behind, a project can get lost. This can result in scope items being included or taken away for the wrong reasons, or quality being compromised, which then has an impact on the project outcome.

In extreme cases, without a shared purpose you could end up with something COMPLETELY DIFFERENT from what you first intended. And then everyone wonders what went wrong. The truth is that nothing specific went wrong. A series of poor decisions were made that were not in line with the project's shared vision, resulting in a bad outcome.

An agreed, up-front shared purpose significantly helps to avoid these kinds of issues. Coming up with an agreed shared purpose is not easy, but it is worthwhile and saves you a world of pain.

Project Vision

The project vision and shared purpose are best agreed on up front using one of my favourite Agile values: collaboration. A shared purpose is not reached by handing around a 60-page business case from one person to another. It is achieved through a genuine conversation between the project's key stakeholders. There is more on how to choose these stakeholders in the next chapter; however, in short they must be people who are critical to the project's success, preferably with what is known as 'skin in the game'. People who care about the outcome of the project. These people will either benefit from the project's success or feel pain if the project fails.

Agreement around the room is all the 'sign-off' you need and this happens when either the project sponsor convinces everyone that their 'dream' is the way to go, or the stakeholders have input into the 'dream' and tweaks are made to ensure everyone is aligned and on board. The more conversation the better at this point, as this will help to identify potential problems later in the project. If you get stuck, it's a good idea to start a question with 'Wouldn't it be great if ...?' and see what comes out next.

I always like to ask people what they are most looking forward to about the project. This encourages people to be honest and curious, and at the same time ecological, considering others outside of themselves. Curiosity is great and means people ask more questions, which will greatly assist in getting to the Why. In fact, the more you ask 'why?' or 'for what purpose?' the better at this point. For example, 'Why are we using Agile to do this project?' There are no limitations here except the limitations you place on yourself.

The shared purpose is a great thing to have written on a wall, in your signature block and at your desk, to remind you and others of why you are doing what you are doing and the difference you will make. This helps during decision-making, as having a known and clear purpose means decisions are easy and effortless. It is also enduring and can help during tough times – which, of course, we know projects have.

Project Elevator Pitch

THE ELEVATOR PITCH...

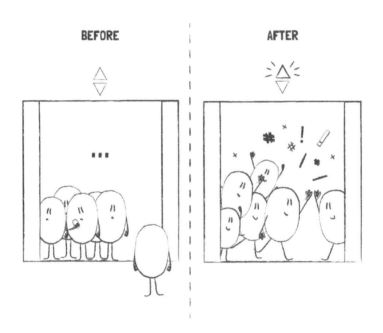

Another great way to reach a project vision that the team can share and use to keep on track is to agree on a project elevator pitch. This is a short message that clearly states the Why of the project, a statement that all the team can get behind and communicate in a short elevator ride. A great elevator pitch conveys purpose and at the same time leaves the listener wanting more.

A great example of an elevator pitch is: "My team is working on an exciting project to help our customers find our recipes on their mobile phones while shopping for ingredients in the supermarket."

From a change management standpoint, a team that is speaking in the same language is worth its weight in gold. Consistent messaging that is on purpose not only gets the word out, but also strengthens the message and keeps the team striving towards a common goal. The exact wording of elevator pitches may vary between the stakeholders that you and your team encounter so that no matter who they are, the project vision means something to them.

"Vision without action is merely a dream. Action without vision just passes the time. Vision with action can change the world."

Joel A. Barker

Trust

A conversation about shared vision and purpose, about the Why, is not complete without exploring the concept of trust. When you are in the process of defining the project vision, having trust in your team and in yourself is critical, because many project visions sound big to start with and the How is not immediately obvious. In fact, this is why many people want to rush to the How, because they will not feel safe until they know all the steps to get to the end.

Know that you are going to work out the How and it is not to be worried about now. You and your trusted team will get to it

– but not right now. Without trust in yourself, your stakeholders and your team, you will never get started.

Trust in your team is one of the key Agile principles. In fact, the answer to many issues that come up during an Agile project is 'Let's take it to the team'. No one is expected to be an island. And I argue that without trust in yourself, you will never trust your team. In fact, in most cases where a leader does not trust the people around them, this simply means they have no trust in themselves.

Does that sound like someone you know? I'm sure we all have a story we can share here.

Putting This into Practice – the hierarchy of ideas

The hierarchy of ideas is a concept from neuro-linguistic programming (NLP) and is a powerful tool to help increase your flexibility of thought. You see, in the process of coming up with a shared vision, everyone is going to start from a different place. Some stakeholders are thinking very high level, abstract even. Other stakeholders want to understand the detail, the How. And yet other stakeholders are excitedly thinking about 'what else' might be possible.

All these people have a place in your project. It's important that you know how to recognise them and use their ideas appropriately. I have put together a model for you called the *Agile Project Manager* hierarchy of ideas. Here's how to use it.

Step 1. Start with the Why. Allow the project sponsor to fully articulate their dream. Do not interrupt. Now is not the time to poke holes in it and come up with ideas as to why it might not be possible. The dream is still being built and conveyed. All questions at this point must have positive intent and build on the dream. If the purpose is not clear, great questions to ask are 'What is the purpose of ...?' and 'What will that lead to?' Keep asking until the vision is fully and easily understood.

Step 2. There will be enthusiastic business stakeholders at this point who might have other ideas. Once the dream is built (and only then), it's great to have a 'what else' conversation. You see, now that you have a purpose, there could be a number of different vehicles for achieving that purpose. A simple example: you decide you need shoes. What is the purpose of shoes? Explore high enough and you could end up with purposes like 'happiness', 'joy' or 'pain-free ambulatory activities'. Ask enough people and you will find that everyone has a different purpose for shoes. How else could you then achieve that purpose? There may be other options than shoes that might work for you. The great thing about asking 'what else?' is that it opens your mind to the possibility of there being something else. You might not think there is, but you never know if you can benchpress that 60 kg weight until you lie down on the bench and apply effort (with a qualified spotter of course ...).

Step 3. THEN talk about the How. Now that the dream is built and options discussed, now AND ONLY NOW talk about how it might be achieved. Start this too early and the vision might not be understood, the purpose might not be articulated in a way that everyone gets. But once the dream is built and the options discussed, this is when you let the 'detail' people into the room. Up to this point, they have been waiting anxiously outside or sitting inside the room trying to remain quiet while eyeing off the catering cart. Now is the time for the detailed steps, the technology, the tools: all the options that support the agreed vision.

You will notice that there is a spot where you feel more comfortable in the hierarchy of ideas. Although I have placed the project sponsor, enthusiastic business stakeholders and project team in certain places, this is based on general experience. I have also come across project sponsors so deep in the detail that I have had to ask 'for what purpose?' a number of times before we understood the project purpose. And project teams can be just as much across the shared purpose of their project as they are across the details.

The more efficiently you can combine the knowledge and experience of your stakeholders, wherever they sit in the hierarchy of ideas, the better they will contribute to, understand and act on the project vision.

Where do you sit? Where are you most comfortable having a conversation? Notice where that is and ask yourself what questions you need to be able to answer in order to move easily and effortlessly around the hierarchy of ideas. The truly Agile PM can operate everywhere in the hierarchy of ideas, moving seamlessly between each step and maximising input from a range of stakeholders.

SPONSOR = big picture

STAKEHOLDERS = other ideas

TEAM = details

"We cannot solve our problems with the same thinking
we used when we created them."

Albert Einstein

Project Success = Team Success = Personal Success

So, now you have thought about your own purpose. In doing
that, you are in a stronger position to ensure your project
sponsor has clearly articulated their vision to the project team.
Armed with this shared purpose, you are now able to easily
navigate your way around the hierarchy of ideas between
the sponsor's vision, the stakeholders' input and your team's
implementation.

Because of this skill, you can help your team, with the assistance of your stakeholders, start to articulate and communicate what success for YOUR project looks like. Ensure this is in words that everyone can understand and identify with. You might even want to come up with your project elevator pitch. This is your and your team's way of easily and consistently letting everyone know why you are doing your project and the value it is bringing to the organisation. It will not only help people identify with the work you are doing, but help them take action.

Chapter Summary:

- Knowing your own purpose is key to your success. Ensure that you know the purpose of everything you do.
- A shared vision for your project is critical. Ensure that you reach it through authentic conversation and collaboration.
- Use the hierarchy of ideas to increase your flexibility of thought.
- Trust your team. Trust yourself first.
- Build self-efficacy by pushing out of your comfort zone into your growth zone.
- Whenever you learn something new, teach it to someone else!

... Or What's in It for Me?

Now, before you go and skip this chapter because it seems a bit negative, listen up. I understand. We spent the last chapter together talking about knowing your Why and understanding your purpose, and it was kind of inspirational, wasn't it? Focusing on everything that could go wrong seems like a bit of a downer, right?

Wrong. This is exactly where you need to be.

A vision is a wonderful thing. It focuses you and your team on the most important part of the project. It serves as the guiding light to ensure everyone stays on track. And people stay focused on the guiding light as long as they know their own needs are being taken care of. But there are still a number of people (more than you think) who are experiencing fear. Fear of the unknown. Fear of change. The issue with these people is that they could derail your project before it even starts. The great thing about these people is that they can actively contribute to discovering all the things that could go wrong in your project. These people have a place.

However, in this chapter we're not only talking about anticipating everything that can go wrong; we are also talking about setting your project up so it goes as smoothly as possible. Just because you have brainstormed everything that could go wrong, this does not mean the project will be easy.

But it can be, if you approach risk with an optimistic and creative outlook.

Some years ago, I was moving house. Everything was going smoothly. The move had been well planned and executed. Boxes were packed and the truck almost loaded. There were a few items remaining here or there that were still to go. Anxious to get to my new home, I sent the truck ahead, saying I'd just pick up those final things and drive over in my car.

Three car trips later, I was done. And exhausted. You see, by not anticipating how much stuff I really had left and how long it would take to drive to my new home in my car, I had suddenly turned what could have been an easy move into a drama. Melbourne peak-hour traffic is not to be messed with. How did I not anticipate this when I had planned so well?

To fully understand this, it's best to start with why risk exists in the first place.

Why Risk?

Firstly, as humans we tend to be overly optimistic and this is often referred to as 'optimism bias'. According to Tali Sharot in her 2012 TED Talk, 80% of us suffer from the cognitive illusion that gives us the tendency to overestimate the possibility of good events in our lives and underestimate the likelihood of bad events. Sharot states: "We are more optimistic than realistic". Also, we LOVE to create drama. Many of the problems in our lives are of our own making. We have caused them or at least played a large part in them.

Why do we create drama? Why do risks even eventuate in the first place? Let's explore this in two ways.

1. Focus

Firstly, our laser-like focus can get us into trouble. We become so focused on one thing (like moving into our new house) that we fail to see other things which might need our attention, but are not as obvious. One of my favourite rules of human behaviour is:

> *What you focus on, you get more of ...*
> *to the exclusion of everything else.*

Do you see how this can be awesome? Once focused on a goal, we are bound to achieve it when we can keep our focus. Think of an elite athlete preparing for the Olympic Games. The double-edged sword with this one is 'to the exclusion of everything else'. Great news if 'everything else' is not relevant. Bad news if it is. And in the case of projects (and most things we do in life), it most likely is VERY relevant. We simply cannot afford for our optimism to blind us.

2. Variety

Our need for variety, excitement and difference makes us who we are, but also makes us overlook risks or almost unconsciously invite them into our lives. Projects can sometimes feel a bit 'been there, done that' or 'same old, same old'. If this is how you are feeling, I strongly suggest that you find another project.

Every project should feel different and offer you an exciting new opportunity to make a difference. It is when things feel dull or mundane that we seek variety in sometimes unresourceful and dangerous ways. I am all for exploring new things, but not when this exposes my project or my team to unnecessary risks.

Why so Early?

A project that I helped with a few years ago had an offshore development team, but was recruiting an iteration manager within Australia. The iteration manager (a role name derived from Extreme Programming and sometimes referred to as the 'Scrum Master', which is a Scrum term) coordinates the team on a day-to-day basis and is critical in managing the output of the team (e.g. development code). The iteration manager protects the team and ensures it is not overloaded AND is doing the work it needs to do.

Leaving the development team without this coordination point locally was a recipe for disaster. I'm not saying the project would not work, but I am saying it could have been harder than it needed to be. Calling the potential risk out early allowed us to explore the option of having an iteration manager located offshore – close to the team. Not calling it out could have resulted in problems as the project got started and prevented us from meeting one of the most critical Agile principles and that is to satisfy the customer through early delivery.

Risks are about identifying not only points of failure, but also items that could make the project more challenging than it needs to be.

My house move wasn't a failure because I did not identify just how many items I would need to drive over in my car after the truck left. It was still a success. But by failing to identify the risk of leaving items behind instead of packing them in the truck, I made the house move harder than it needed to be.

No one really wants to make life harder for themselves. But unconsciously we do make it harder. We can't help it. Our need to focus on success, coupled with our need for variety in our lives, is a powerful force. To counteract this force, we need to focus on what really matters and achieve variety in ways that are resourceful and sustainable. This avoids (or at least mitigates) the risk pitfall, allowing us to power through a difficult situation.

The Whole of Life Model

Before we look at types of risk, it might be a good opportunity to introduce a concept of Rob Thomsett's called the Whole of Life Model. Rob Thomsett is a well-known author and presenter on the subject of people and project management. His books *Third Wave Project Management: A Handbook for Managing the Complex Information Systems for the 1990s*, *Radical Project Management* and *The Agile Project Manager's Toolkit* are well known by many of Australia's largest organisations which have benefited from his knowledge and interactive workshops.

The Whole of Life Model, shown here, is great to have at the top of our minds when planning any change. It encourages the project practitioner to think of their project not only from the delivery point of view (bottom left quadrant), but also from the viewpoint of the support (business and technology) after going live and the all-important benefits realisation phase. The Agile principles of sustainable development and technical excellence underpin this model.

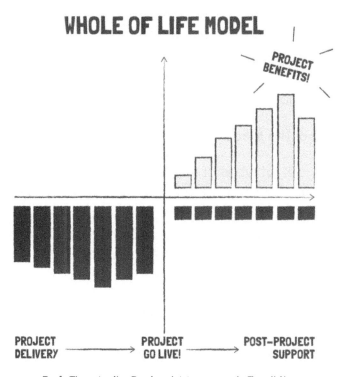

WHOLE OF LIFE MODEL

PROJECT BENEFITS!

PROJECT DELIVERY → PROJECT GO LIVE! → POST-PROJECT SUPPORT

Ref: *The Agile Project Manager's Toolkit*
Rob & Camille Thomsett, 2009

With the Whole of Life model in mind, let's look at risk in a bit more detail.

Types of Risk

Project execution risk – this is everything that can go wrong during the course of the delivery of your project. These are the easiest risks to come up with, as many of them are similar to (or the same as) risks you have either encountered before or mitigated against in previous projects. They could be as simple as the risk of hardware not arriving in time from a vendor or as complex as the inability of the team to solve a difficult technical problem.

Delivered risk – this is everything that could go wrong as a result of your project being successful. What are you changing that could have an adverse impact on business as usual? These risks will eventuate after the project finishes and are therefore harder to predict than project execution risks, but providing you have the right people in the conversation (see Chapter 3 for more on this), you should get all your answers. When your project is successful, what will change for the business or technology teams? What might they have to do differently as a result?

Benefits realisation risk – this is everything that could go wrong after the project deliverables are completed and the project sponsor and stakeholders are in the process of realising benefits. Like delivered risk, these are risks that eventuate after project completion and are dependent on factors outside the project team's direct control. What could go wrong that might mean the business does not realise the (financial or non-financial) benefits you anticipated? This is another challenging conversation, as often the PM is not around for benefits realisation. For example, much of the benefits realisation activity might depend on the sales team selling the new product your project has built. A benefit realisation risk could be the risk that the sales team does not have enough people to do this or may not understand the product fully enough to sell it. The earlier this is understood the better, as it could mean the difference between the project being a monumental success or not going ahead at all.

Personal risk – this is a different way to think about risk, introduced to me by Rob Thomsett. Even though the chance of a project being successful is high and the benefits will be great, what risk is there to you personally? Is this something you can REALLY do? What compromises will you have to make personally? To your relationships? To your health? I once worked with a PM who took on a major compliance project – just at the time in his life when he was ready to dial back to three days a week and focus on his property and family, located an hour out of the city. The personal risk of this project was a lot higher to him that it might have been to someone who lived nearer to the city and was prepared to work five days a week (and was perhaps single with no kids). Personal risk counts but is often overlooked. When you think about it, personal risk is mostly commonsense, it's just not commonly applied. Your ability to assess a project's personal risk to you is the difference between getting the so-called 'lucky' projects and not.

Personal Motivation

We are all motivated by different things and it's important to understand how your team members and stakeholders are motivated before you assess risk. All of us have various traits that define us. It's simply the way we are and it's the way we approach the world. The terms 'glass half empty' versus 'glass half full' is referring to what is known as a meta-program. In his book, *Unlimited Power – the new science of personal achievement*, Tony Robbins says:

"All human behavior revolves around the urge to gain pleasure or avoid pain. You pull away from a lighted match in order to avoid the pain of burning your hand. You sit and watch a beautiful sunset because you get pleasure from the glorious celestial show as day glides into night."

Some people are more motivated by moving towards pleasure. Others are more motivated by moving away from pain. We can all be a bit of both. It's important to ensure that when planning for risk, you are considering both these motivations and have both types of people in the room. Can you imagine running a risk workshop full of just one type of person? I'll let you think about which scenario would be worse – a room full of only towards-motivated people or a room full of only away-motivated people ...

How to Put This All into Practice

A great way to start putting this all into practice is getting everyone in the team, including the key stakeholders, to brainstorm their 'hopes and fears'. I like this language, as 'risk' means different things to different people. All this brainstorming takes is two pieces of butchers paper and a bunch of sticky notes. But first, set the scene. Ensure the project vision is within sight of the team – perhaps written up on a whiteboard. Begin by introducing the purpose of the get-together and why it is important to understand what could go wrong not only for preventing bad things from happening, but also for making sure the project runs as easily and smoothly as possible. This may get a few laughs ('what project goes easily and smoothly?'), but it is a sneaky way of ensuring you are both appealing to the people who look for what could go wrong and also not isolating the people who are more positive in nature and less keen to talk about the negatives. It's also important to let people know that what they write can be anonymous if they choose; however, encourage open discussions wherever possible.

Give everyone at least five minutes to write down all their hopes and fears for the project. If people laugh and chat, that's okay. This exercise can make people uneasy at first and they may need to let off steam by cracking jokes. Then get everyone to stick their thoughts up on the butchers paper. While people continue to chat, read through the sticky notes and add your own. Then group these into some logical groups, such as project execution, benefits realisation, operational, personal, customer etc. You may find groupings unique to your project. Invite people up to read the sticky notes and then discuss:

- How did everyone find the exercise?

- What are some of the themes?

- Are there any surprises?

- Is anything not clear?

Then discuss some actions:

- What risks can we avoid?

- What risks can we pass onto another project or team?

- What risks can we mitigate against and how?

- What risks do we have to accept?

The Power of the Placebo

I recently read an article in *Runner's World* (February 2014) about a test that researchers in Taiwan ran on a group of athletes. Half of the group was given a pill and told it was a multi-vitamin, while the other half was given a pill and told it was a placebo. Both groups were actually given placebos. They were then asked to complete a number of tests, including using a pedometer. Dramatically different outcomes ensued. Those who were told they'd been given a multi-vitamin were more likely to walk a shorter route and choose unhealthy foods. It appeared that because they thought they were taking a supplement, those athletes unconsciously felt it literally 'supplemented' their training.

The same goes for projects. Many project teams that spend time evaluating and setting up actions for managing risks still go on to have issues because they fail to follow through. Risk brainstorming can be seen as the placebo for good project management. It's the equivalent of buying a headache tablet, then not taking it and wondering why you still have your headache.

Discussing risk is no replacement for good risk management and follow-up actions, including regular meetings to discuss updates, must be undertaken in order for risks to continue to be managed. These meetings can get dull at times – a great Agile PM makes them as interesting and interactive as possible.

Some ways to ensure the team focuses on risk and follow-up:

- Don't wait until the regular risk meeting to follow up the team's actions – instead, take time to meet with people individually and ask how they are going with their actions. This can be less confronting than asking them in a room full of people.

- 'Gamify' the risk meeting, with points awarded for risks closed and actions taken. This is a great way of encouraging people to follow up and close risk items.

- Schedule the risk meeting for when people can be present and pay attention. 4 pm on a Friday is not an ideal time – assess different times and environments and find a timing and location to suit your team. This gets more attention and shows the team you are putting some thought into it.

Opportunities

In the midst of thinking about all the things that could go wrong and planning your mitigations, it is worth thinking about all the things that could go RIGHT. What I mean here is that unexpected opportunities could come up and you want to be in the best position to take advantage of them.

While a risk might be: 'Funding cuts due to an upcoming restructure may result in reducing scope and decreasing benefits' ...

... an opportunity might be: 'With the increased focus on digitalisation, the project may receive more attention and funding, resulting in more features being added, increasing benefits'. If this came to pass, what would you do?

This is not about being overly optimistic; it's about being able to take advantage of good things when they happen – such as increased funding or attention – in the same way that you want to be placed to mitigate against bad things such as decreased funding.

In Chapter 4, we're going to talk more about scope, which ultimately leads to a product 'backlog' in Agile terms. As an Agile team quickly learns, the product backlog can become overlong and so not everything ends up being done. A great tool I have used with success is an innovation log, where every entry starts with the sentence: 'Wouldn't it be great if ...?' As a project continues, people will have great ideas. Rather than simply adding them to the backlog or putting them through rigorous change control too early, start a separate log that can be assessed by the project sponsor and product owner and then added to the backlog in a more organised fashion.

An innovation log is also a sneaky way of ensuring you only add scope items that have involved the team and critical stakeholders in a collaborative process – that is, they have been well thought out and discussed. This ensures visibility as early as possible, so the team is ready when things go wrong.

The Power of the Reframe

On a project, things go wrong. Quite a lot. A great tool to use when things go wrong, or when people think they are going wrong, is the reframe. A reframe is a way of looking at an issue differently by putting a new perspective, or frame, on thoughts about a situation. This can change the meaning of the situation or problem and create new opportunities to solve it.

A reframe is more than just 'thinking positive'. It involves thinking about something problematic in a way that may shed more light on the solution. The basis of reframing is separating intention from behaviour. There are two ways you can reframe an issue:

- Content – discover additional content that may change the focus or meaning of an event. When discussing a risk or an issue that has happened, ask 'What else do we need to know in order to solve this?' Often our inability to solve a problem comes down to lack of knowledge or resources. Uncovering this knowledge allows a fresh perspective and so a greater chance of the issue being resolved. In some cases you may not be able to find additional meaning easily, so simply ask the question: 'What other meaning could this situation have?' For example, a team member may be behaving in a certain way that is annoying to you and others, so asking this question or perhaps even looking for the positive value in the behaviour is a way of reframing from a content perspective.

- Context – change the context of the situation by taking an undesired attribute and putting it into a different situation where it could be more valuable. For example, a problem may arise in a project such as the wrong IT hardware arriving. A context reframe would ask the question: 'In what situation (i.e. which other project) could this be useful?' This can discover a way of using the issue to your advantage – in this case, locating someone who might benefit from the issue or finding another way to deal with the issue.

I love that one of the key Agile concepts applied in Agile projects is 'take it to the team'. This makes a reframe so much easier. You see, when you're still sitting at your desk at 9 pm trying to work on a problem, the only person working on it is YOU. By taking a challenge to a team of up to nine people (the ideal size for an Agile team or Scrum team), you are opening up the opportunity for the problem to be solved by people who are able to either change the context or add more content. Either way, the problem will be solved much more quickly than if you work on it alone. The saying 'a problem shared is a problem halved' can literally be put into action. If your team has eight people (this number makes the maths easier – you get the idea), then you have taken something and halved it three times. Imagine how much easier the problem will be to reframe, and ultimately overcome, than if it was just up to you to solve.

Recovering from 'Failure'

Okay, something has gone wrong. A risk has become an issue. You have worked at reframing it and found a solution to solve it. Or you're at least well on the way. The risk was anticipated and planned for to some degree, but at the end of the day it doesn't look great for you and your team. The BEST way to move forward from this point is to remember:

There is no failure, only feedback.

This is a type of reframe, in a way. When we think of something that has gone wrong from the viewpoint of 'failure', we have labelled it in a way that is unresourceful. How we label it does not change anything. What's done is done. However, the way we label it may affect how the team acts going forward.

A great Agile PM simple labels it 'feedback' and works with the team to move forward. The entrepreneur/inventor Thomas

Edison once spoke of the thousand-plus times he "failed" to invent the light bulb:

> "I have not failed. I've just found ten thousand ways that don't work."
>
> Thomas A. Edison

Imagine if Edison had thought of even one of his unsuccessful attempts as a failure. At this very moment, you are probably benefiting from the outcome of Edison not labelling his early attempts failure.

Your project may not invent a product that will benefit all of humanity for hundreds of years, but think of the impact of not delivering because you chose to think of a setback as failure. It is simply feedback. Use it as an opportunity to learn and move forward.

Most importantly, ensure that feedback is contained to the iteration, or the piece of work immediately affected, and that the only thing you take forward into future iterations (or projects) is the learning.

Your project retrospectives are a great way of capturing learnings. A retrospective involves the team taking time to reflect on their most recent work. They examine what went well, what did not go well and what they are going to do differently next time to improve. It is an open, honest conversation focused on getting the best outcome for the team. Ensure you create a safe environment so the team feels they can speak openly about what went wrong and what they have learned. Use the feedback as leverage for learning and then move forward.

Chapter Summary:

- You know why risk exists – we're human! And we have our own interests at heart.

- You know how to predict risks:

    o Brainstorm 'hopes and fears'.

- You know how to come up with new ideas for making your project as easy as possible.

- You know some tools to use when risks eventuate:

    o Reframe

    o Take it to the team

    o There is no failure, only feedback.

CHAPTER THREE

... Or Who is on your side?

You now have a project vision – a clear reason for doing your project that you can articulate clearly. You have started to understand your project's risks and what to do about them. You also have some plans in place to take advantage of opportunities as they come up – as we saw in the previous chapter, risk is not only focused on the 'glass half empty' perspective.

This chapter is all about your team: the people you are going to rely on to a certain extent to achieve a successful project outcome. One of the principles that underpins the value of "individuals and interactions over processes and tools" is the team and stakeholders working together daily throughout the project. Agile encourages face-to-face conversation wherever possible, as it is proven to get the best results.

As I'm writing this, my husband is at the stove, putting the final touches on our dinner for tonight. I am so grateful for how supportive he is with things like that. It's when I'm writing that he really steps up to do things around the house. This allows me lots of space and time to think and create. You see, my husband is on my team.

We're going to talk about setting up your project team for success and as we do this, we'll think about who else you may need on your team, outside your project and work situation, to give you all the support you need to be successful in anything – your project, a career or fitness goal, life.

Your Project Team

If you are lucky enough to be selecting your own project team, first do a happy dance and then ask yourself – what is it you are looking for? Are there particular skill sets that are critical to the project's success? How can you go about finding people with those skill sets?

This is the first, obvious step – some other questions to ask yourself when setting up your team are:

- What skills and experience are critical for getting the project done?
- What skills and experience do I need because I don't have them?
- What skills and experience do I need because, while I have them, I won't have time to use them?
- What am I not good at that I need to recruit to fill that gap?
- What sorts of attitudes, beliefs and behaviours am I looking for?
- What personality attributes am I looking for?
- What values do I want the team to hold true to?

Going back to my moving house example, picking a removalist that was capable, friendly and reasonably priced were musts for me. Add a few supportive friends available to help out – moving team done!

Years ago, I was running a project in London that involved going out to almost every station and office of the London Underground (the Tube). I knew I had strengths in coordination and organisation, but I also knew I did not have superpowers. I needed someone similar to me who could do the things I did not have time to do in terms of coordination and communication across the vast Tube network. They did not need to have the same level of project management skills, but they needed to match my energy, enthusiasm and ability to manage a cross-functional remote team. I almost needed a mini-me. I also recognised that my ability to concentrate on detail was limited, especially when I was tired. I knew I needed someone who would persist with sometimes tedious tasks that were necessary in order to get the project across the line. I almost needed an anti-me. With this in mind, I reviewed CVs and interviewed candidates, and ended up hiring an exceptional person who met and exceeded my expectations. What this taught me was the importance of identifying key skills that are not only technical, but personal as well.

Your ability to identify the skill sets required for your project is key to your success. It's worth taking the time at the beginning of the project to think this through. Perhaps a resource risk came up when brainstorming risks? Perhaps a concern was raised when talking through the initial vision – who and what were critical to success? Who or what can we get away without having? Is there anything we can outsource to a specialist who has skills that are hard to find? If we were to do that, what would be some of the risks?

Your Project Stakeholders

In my well thought-out (but frankly naive) honours thesis written in 1994, I proposed that adopting a methodology to select stakeholders for an initiative and involving them early would lead to an increased chance of project success. I cited a number of examples where this did happen and things went well, and a few examples where it didn't happen and things did not go well. I felt that I proved my point somewhat.

Having delivered a number of projects since then and along the way having adopted a number of methods to identify all my stakeholders, I now believe the one thing that holds true is that you can never fully guarantee you have captured all of your stakeholders. Ever.

The most successful method I have used is asking a series of questions. These can be potentially irritating, so use them with care:

- Who stands to benefit the most when this project is successful?
- Who needs to do something to ensure the project delivers benefits?
- Who would complain the most if this project did not go ahead?
- Who would complain first if this project did not go ahead?
- Who could potentially be disadvantaged if this project is successful? How might they need to change? How could we mitigate this?
- Who would celebrate the most if this project did not go ahead?
- Who else?
- Who else?

Now you may think I'm including the last two 'Who else?' for dramatic effect. In fact, I'm not. By simply asking the question 'Who else?' (or 'What else?') you are presupposing that there IS someone (or something) else to consider. There might not be and that's okay. But opening up the possibility that there MAY be someone else ensures that the person you are asking really thinks about it.

Questions like:

- There's not anyone else, is there?

- Is there anyone else?

… close the unconscious mind down and the listener will not think of anyone, and so you may have missed an opportunity to discover that critical person who could make or break your project. Stay open to the possibilities and fully exercise the horizontal axis of the hierarchy of ideas that we explored in Chapter 1.

A project that I helped to get started some time ago thought it had identified all the key stakeholders before I came in to run a workshop. I asked some questions like the ones I suggest above. I definitely approached with care, because according to them this had all been thought out. I encountered a bit of resistance, but hit the jackpot when I asked 'Who would complain first if the project did not go ahead?' Voila, a new stakeholder. And an important one at that.

Don't be afraid to ask these questions. It is your right as a professional project manager or facilitator of change to ensure you know as much as you can that will benefit the eventual outcome of the project. Remember that in Chapter 1, we established how important it is to ask 'Why?' Don't be afraid to ask the questions that need to be asked. Somewhere out there, someone is silently thanking you.

Dealing with Difficult Stakeholders

Every project has these and your project is no exception. I wanted to call this section 'How to turn even the most difficult stakeholder into a raving fan', but we know that in many cases this is near impossible. I suggest two strategies before rushing out to invite your adversaries for coffee. I have named these:

1. Commitment first

2. Focus on your fans

Commitment First

Beckhard and Pritchard (1992) developed a way of thinking about analysing commitment that I have found very helpful in managing my stakeholders. It is called the commitment chart. It encourages you to list your stakeholders or stakeholder groups and identify what you need from each of them in order to build a critical mass to accomplish the change. Do you need them to:

- Make it happen
- Help it happen
- Let it happen (by not blocking)

It is also useful to plot their current level of commitment. For example, you may have a stakeholder that you have classified as needed to 'make it happen', yet your needs assessment places them in 'let it happen'. This is a large gap. The idea here is to find the biggest gaps and prioritise them.

Here is an example of a commitment chart from the start of a project of mine from some time ago (the names have been changed). 'O' is where the stakeholders needed to be and 'X' is where they currently were. As you can see, there were a few stakeholders with significant gaps between these. In fact, two stakeholders were needed to 'make it happen', but had 'no commitment' to the success of the change. Fortunately, a number of their peers were committed to 'help it happen', so there were a number of opportunities to close the gaps and influence those stakeholders to participate in a way that meant success for the project.

Key stakeholders	No commitment	Let it happen	Help it happen	Make it happen
Stephen Black (project sponsor)		XO		
Mary Rose (key stakeholder)				XO
Sumi Krishna (in Mary's team)			XO	
Suman Vin (technology)	X		O	
Gary Kip (technology)	X		O	
Andrew Bentley (technology)	X			O
Tyler Durden (external expert)			XO	
X = Current O = Desired				

Ref: *Changing the Essence* Beckhard & Pritchard (1992)

An important point to note is that 'let it happen' is not a bad thing. It could only be labelled bad if the stakeholder in question needed to 'make it happen'. Having a number of stakeholders 'let it happen' is a good thing – in fact, having too many stakeholders 'make it happen' could be an issue in itself.

I love this commitment chart tool because it makes the potentially complex simple. When you have completed it, I encourage you to keep this table to yourself or share it only with a few trusted advisers. The stakeholder commitment issues that could arise from a person inadvertently picking up the table from the printer and seeing your assessment of them are not worth thinking about.

Focus on Your Fans

In Simon Sinek's book *Start with Why*, he draws on what he calls the law of diffusion of innovations. The diffusion of innovations is a theory that explains the rate at which new ideas and technology spread. It was made popular by Everett Rogers in his book *Diffusion of Innovations*. This theory is great for agents of change, because our aim for change is to have it accepted and we work to spread it through a number of channels, ultimately leading to it becoming self-sustaining once reaching critical mass.

According to the diffusion of innovations theory, there are five types of adopters of change:

- innovators
- early adopters
- early majority
- late majority
- laggards.

Sinek encourages the reader to focus on the innovators and the early adopters, because the majority is not interested unless someone else owns the product or is doing the new thing. Rob Thomsett uses this theory consistently: he finds his fans, focuses on them, then uses them as advocates to move the masses. Apple listens to its fans and makes products that appeal to people who are willing to sleep overnight outside an Apple store in order to get the latest product. I've never seen an Apple advertisement designed to convince Android users to convert.

The thing I love about this approach is that it's very freeing. By focusing on the people who already 'love your work', you can turn them into advocates who will move the majority for you. The majority will ultimately tip the balance. Investing time in the laggards, the people who are actively resisting, is simply not worth it. This does not mean they are to be ignored. The key to success when focusing on your fans is ensuring that they are actually advocates and not just simply enjoying the fruits of your labour without sharing.

I recommend using a combination of both approaches. Understand the gaps first, identify your raving fans and turn them into advocates. Then make sure you face the potential disruptive elements of your stakeholder group. After all, some stakeholders cannot be ignored.

In the commitment chart example above, I started by understanding the commitment level of my stakeholders and working on my fans first, using them as advocates to convince the stakeholders without commitment to get involved. It wasn't easy and there were a few bumps in the road, but ultimately, the time you invest is worth it.

Don't Make It Personal

It can be easy to interpret a stakeholder's actions as some kind of personal attack. They could be aggressive in meetings or downright rude. I once thought a particular stakeholder disliked me, even after people assured me 'It's just her way, don't take it personally'. Months after the project ended, I found myself chatting to her on a social occasion. As it turned out, she had just gone through a bitter divorce. She even went so far as to say she had enjoyed working with me. Wow!

This is not to say that people won't dislike you. The key is:

Nothing has meaning but the meaning you give it.

Don't assign meaning. Chances are, unless you are a talented mind-reader, you're probably wrong.

Relationships before Everything Else

During my first week in my first project coaching role, I had the opportunity to listen to one of the top executives speak. It was a general update, but he also shared some personal stories, touching on time management. I asked him what some of his strategies were for getting everything done. After all, his calendar was filled back to back and every meeting required some pre-reading. How did he do it? His answer surprised me. He owned up to the fact that he didn't always get around to doing all the pre-reading and often had to let people down by not being able to attend meetings as expected.

He said the key to all this was to build great relationships of trust. Because, inevitably, there comes a time when you have to let someone down by either declining a meeting or not being able to help them. There comes a time when you have to say no. When you have a great relationship built on trust, this letdown is not as big a deal. If there is no trust, it's a much bigger deal and sometimes unrecoverable. The executive said he prioritised building relationships over everything else, especially administrative duties. He even went so far as to say that a measure of my success was going to be how often he saw me downstairs having coffee with people. What a job!

There's always time to update a project schedule or craft that perfect email. So seize those precious moments to stop by the desk of a team member, colleague or stakeholder instead, and save hours of time and potential angst later.

RELATIONSHIP BUILDING

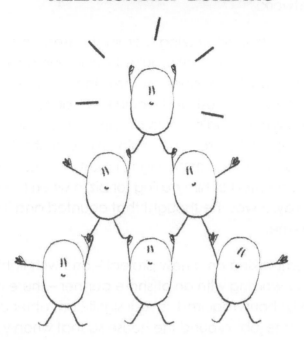

Your Own Team

Early in this chapter, I mentioned my husband and how supportive he is, especially when my head is down, working hard. You may well have a fantastic project team and engaged sponsors, but a support network outside of work is also important. This network could include:

- your significant other
- your family
- your extended family
- your friends
- your ex-colleagues.

All these people (and others) are people you can sign onto your team at the start of (or during) any project. You don't have to call them into a meeting or anything like that, but it's worth working to understand what you might need in a support network.

Not long ago, I started working a project based an hour's travel away from home that required some long hours as the project got going. It was good to know that as I often arrived home after 8 pm, my husband would have done some shopping for dinner and it would be almost ready when I came in the door. Before you envision him in a chef's hat cooking gourmet meals every night, I must confess sometimes that 'help' consisted of him calling for pizza when I was 20 minutes away. It was the thought that counted and it meant so much to me.

If you are embarking on a new project – one with tight deadlines or working with an offshore partner – there might be late (or early) hours required. Is your significant other up to taking on some jobs around the house so that when you drag yourself home late in the evening, there's food to eat and an understanding ear?

Also, consider your friends and their skills and experience. How might they be able to assist you in your role? I am lucky to have some very clever friends and, providing I'm not breaking any business confidences, I often run problems past them to get their perspectives. An issue that might be a big deal in my work setting could be a problem that they have solved in the past. Any opportunity to leverage off others' experience is worth taking advantage of.

In another recent project, I was using a lot of new skills in a completely new environment. I contacted a number of people I knew who were practised practitioners and took them out for coffee in order to ask them questions and benefit from their experience.

> "If I have seen further
> it is by standing on ye shoulders of Giants."

> Isaac Newton

Your friends and family are your support network. They are the people you relax with over coffee and wine on the weekend. They obviously care about you or they wouldn't be your friends, so go ahead and tap their skills and enjoy the multiplier effect that results. At best you could solve a complex problem; at worst you have a sympathetic ear (and a nice cup of coffee or glass of wine!)

They are the "giants" Isaac Newton was referring to. Newton did not have the benefit of the internet in his time, but when you think of the people we now have access to thanks to social media compared with even 10 or 20 years ago, the number and availability of 'giants' shoulders' have vastly increased! I often ask a question on social media and am inundated with replies and suggestions (and sometimes more questions – be careful here).

There is now no excuse whatsoever to mull over a problem completely on your own. Find those giants – whether they be your close friends, colleagues or people you have met through Twitter – and stand on their shoulders. In the end, everyone benefits.

Your Engaged Project Sponsor

Your project sponsor, and their level of influence and interest, are key to your success. They are your most important stakeholder and without them on board, you don't have a project. The project sponsor is ultimately responsible for delivering the project benefits. So while you, as the PM, are delivering the scope as agreed, your sponsor should be ensuring that what you are delivering can be turned into the business outcome or benefit that was agreed on at the start of the project. Sometimes you get stuck with a lousy sponsor. Other times you get a gem.

Your sponsor, and their engagement, are more within your control than you may think. And again, this comes down to great questions. Rob Thomsett talks about this extensively in his books and emphasises the importance of a great relationship between project sponsor and PM. The key thing here is: do whatever it takes to meet with your sponsor regularly and elicit from them what is important to them, understanding that every sponsor has different needs. With those needs in mind, we have no idea the pressure our sponsor may be under (who knows what is really going on in their world?), so our ability to show empathy could be the factor that makes the difference. Empathy and a bit of cleverness.

Considering we will have no idea about our sponsor's specific situation, how do we achieve our outcome of getting their engagement? Without turning this into a section on advanced stalking methods, here are some ideas to consider if you are having trouble getting time with your sponsor:

- Find out what time they arrive at work and greet them at the door/carpark
- Befriend their assistant so they work harder to fit you into their boss's calendar
- Call them or swing past their desk on the offchance they will be there (I'm always surprised at how few people are willing to do this)
- Work closely with them to understand what they most need from you and give them that; it can be surprising what they are really after

Also, always be ready to give a short and helpful update on your project at a moment's notice. Your ability to leverage an elevator ride could be the difference between a successful interaction and a missed opportunity.

Dig the Well before You are Thirsty

Just when you think you have it all sorted out with your sponsor, your stakeholders and your friends, here's another stakeholder task to consider. I like to call it 'dig the well before you are thirsty'. While you are busy engaging all the people who are relevant to what you are doing right now, who are the people you COULD be engaging who could be helpful in the future? This is turning out to be some stakeholder list, right?

Not long ago, I found myself unexpectedly out of contract. Organisational priorities had changed and some projects (including mine) were put on hold. I was suddenly not-employed. I was lucky enough to have taken my own advice and fostered some great relationships with my network and kept in regular contact, so I knew who might be able to recommend me for a role. I made some calls, had some coffees and before I knew it, had some great choices.

I'm not sure about you, but I have often been on the end of a 'help me please' email via LinkedIn from someone I haven't interacted with for a long time. Of course I would love to help them, but what was it they did again? What was their recent experience? What work did they prefer? I was also lucky that my network that I kept in contact with were enjoyable people to hang out with. So the effort to contact them was easy.

Your willingness to reach out to your personal network could be the difference between having engaging, interesting projects and being out of work for a long time.

The Power of Your Environment

We can't talk about our friend and family support networks without talking about how the people we surround ourselves with directly affect our results. Are you creating the environment you need in order to be successful?

> "You are the average of the five people
> you spend the most time with."

Jim Rohn

YOU ARE THE AVERAGE OF THE 5 PEOPLE YOU SPEND THE MOST TIME WITH

Check in. How are your five people working out for you? Are they successful, with a positive outlook? Are they people you can go to with problems and they have solutions or at least suggestions? Or are they struggling and complaining all the time? This is not about dumping your friends unless they are millionaires, it is about checking how your environment is working for you.

Simon T. Bailey in his book *Shift Your Brilliance* says:

"We exist in a matrix, or quantum field, that is pulling things toward us like a magnet. We repel from us the things that are incongruent with our worldview. In other words, you will always attract people, situations, and circumstances based on the vibrational energy that you release into the universe."

In other words, if something exists within our environment, we chose for it to be there. If something is not there, it was our choice not to have it there. Bailey even goes so far as to say that we determine the size of our own quantum field. So if we're getting small results, it's because we have chosen a small quantum field that yields small results.

Think of the space you are in right now, while reading this book – whether it be in a room or perhaps outside in a garden. Wherever it is, you have chosen to be there and everything around you is there because you put it there. Unless you're in prison. I'm not trying to be funny here – the reason that we have prisons to punish criminals is to take away all feeling of choice and control. The less control you feel you have over your environment – real or imagined – the more limited your results. And we have so much more control over our environments than we realise.

Chapter Summary:

Your team is bigger than you think! When embarking on any kind of change – from a house move to a large multimillion-dollar program – think of your team. Your WHOLE team. These people are:

- your project team
- your project stakeholders
- stakeholders in the wider business
- your significant other
- your friends
- your family
- your ex-colleagues
- people you meet at conferences or networking events

- people who work in industries or roles that you could be interested in in the future.

Regular contact with these people will ensure that you are not only gainfully and productively employed, but are working on something you love and somewhere you feel you belong. Your team is everything. Don't neglect your relationships.

"The deeper your relationships, the stronger your leadership."

Robin Sharma, *The Leader Who had No Title*

... Or What's the What?

Knowing your project scope, REALLY knowing it, can be the difference between a good Agile PM and an outstanding one. This is the What of your project: what you need to do to ensure your project vision is realised.

By the time it's time to start talking about scope, the project vision is clear, the project sponsor fully on board and engaged, and all key stakeholders known and engaged. It's now time to start talking about the What. As in, 'what's in' and 'what's out'. Just like moving house, when you need to be clear about what you're taking to your new home and what you are letting go in the form of rubbish or charity, a great project scope is clear about what is being done and what is not.

At this point, it's tempting to start talking about the How. 'How will we do this?' 'What methodology should we use?' 'What technology do we need?' etc. Bear with me and know that at some point we will get to that. Talking about the How too early in a project limits thinking, which leads to limited outcomes.

Years ago, I worked with a PM called Jacques. He was running a large compliance program for a financial services institution and I was running one of the smaller related projects. As I investigated my project a little further, I found some additional work that needed doing and looked critical to Jacques's project. I raised it with him, thinking it would become part of his project (after all, it was critical to his success). He deflected the work by influencing the project office to raise a new project and assign a PM. He then raised a dependency on the project.

At first I thought Jacques was not a team player. How hard would it have been to include a few extra scope items in his project? I didn't understand fully until both our projects went live a few months later. You see, Jacques's project finishing on time was his key measure of success due to the regulatory nature of the work. And although this additional work was crucial to his success, it wasn't part of his agreed project scope. He had cleverly put a distinct boundary around his project – he had already defined success and wasn't moving on it. Any additions would have put his project at risk.

Years later, I had the opportunity to put this into practice when I was placed in charge of a pilot for a new voice-recording technology project. Now, I knew the term 'pilot' is vastly misunderstood in most organisations, where it is often understood to mean 'a small rollout with many more rollouts to come'. With that in mind, I defined my scope carefully and identified the sites that would be included in the pilot and those that would not be, noting, of course, which sites would be considered for a rollout if the pilot was successful.

Even with my clearly defined scope and communication to stakeholders, I was put under pressure at every turn to add another site to my pilot ('It won't take that much extra work to include the call centres, right?'). If I had said yes to everyone, the project would have become a multi-year, multimillion-dollar rollout of epic proportions. Okay, a bit of an exaggeration, but it would have been big. And my 'pilot' project would have been a failure.

Saying No

No one likes to say no – especially to someone we want to please. But this was a big lesson for me in saying no and sticking to it. I liken a project to a wheelbarrow with rocks in it. It is the PM's job to push the wheelbarrow along a course and cross the finish line within a certain timeframe. If you put another rock in, it has to go slower. Put yet another rock in, the wheelbarrow slows down again. Put enough rocks in and the wheelbarrow falls over, and no one wins.

So by saying no, even if it displeases people, you are actually doing them a favour in the long run. It gives them the chance to start another wheelbarrow with a better chance of success than your already overloaded one.

Steve Jobs, well known for his intense focus and huge success, often asked his design chief Jony Ive how many times he had said no in a day. Ive claimed (at a *Vanity Fair* New Establishment Summit) that Jobs' view was "the more noes the better" in order to maintain laser-like focus.

Fully understanding and communicating your project scope at the very start makes it easier to keep focused, and to know when to say no and when to say 'of course'. Involving your key stakeholders in this discussion gives them context as to when it might be appropriate to ask for something new or different, and when it's better not to. Transparent, honest conversations as early as possible bring everyone's thoughts to light a lot earlier too – which means you are saying no now, rather than later.

Your Project Scope

A great Agile concept that I love, but that can be misunderstood, is the idea that we do 'just enough'. This isn't being lazy, it's being sensible. The Agile principle refers to this concept as "the art of maximizing the amount of work not done". Good questions to ask at the start are 'What is the minimum we can do to achieve our project vision?' or 'What could we get away without doing and still be considered successful?' Because we've all seen project scope grow like crazy and before we know it, a project is out of control.

The way to prevent this from happening is to always come back to the project vision. A question I love asking sponsors is 'If you could have ONE THING from this project, what would it be? What is the ONE most important thing to you?' A fabulous project sponsor will be very clear on this one thing. This one thing is hopefully the thing that keeps them awake at night and that they desperately want solved. If this is a number of things, what is the one thing that these things lead to? Perhaps there should be a number of projects?

This kind of questioning allows the team and stakeholders to have laser focus when working on a project. Decisions about what is 'in' and what is 'out' become easy, because something either directly leads to the project vision or it doesn't. There may be scope items that are necessary in order for other scope items to be achieved. That's okay too. They must all lead to the project vision.

When I learned this from Rob Thomsett, it made sense of all my previous project successes and failures. I can almost go so far as to say that any project I could remember that had gone badly came down to an unclear vision, while the projects that had gone well had had a very clear vision and as a result, very clear scope.

Rob's tool is called the O3 Model – Outcomes, Outputs and Objectives. Use it at the start of a project when planning scope and review this regularly.

Outcomes: this is the 'end game' or project vision – what is the one thing the project needs to achieve? What is the project's Why?

Outputs: what are the tangible outputs (or scope items) that the project team needs to produce in order to achieve the primary outcome? What are the Whats?

Objectives: what are the activities the project team need to do in order to achieve the outputs? Note: all objectives should start with 'To ...' as they have a 'doing' focus.

It's easy (and happens a lot) to go straight to Objectives. As human beings we can't help ourselves. We love to 'do'. Our longing to 'do' has resulted in the culture of 'busyness' that surrounds us. We are measured on the stream of busy we create through our constant doing, and not as much on the actual outputs at the end, let alone the outcome which is where the real benefits are.

One of the first times I facilitated a workshop using the O3 tool, I had to use my best influencing skills to convince the project sponsor to put down the whiteboard marker in the middle of him writing out all the things he expected the project team to do. It was looking like being a long list. Sitting down to think about the project's Why was a lot more challenging, as it involves asking some challenging questions. But these questions, when answered, make coming up with the outputs and ultimately the 'doing' so much easier.

Be ready to use your best influencing skills here, as asking people questions like these can be perceived as time wasting. Take the time to ask the questions and so much time will be saved later in the project. A great project vision and an understanding of a higher intention make scope conversations easy.

When talking about project scope, it can often be difficult to look too far out into the future. Hence the term 'minimal marketable product' was coined (originally by Mark Denne and Jane Cleland-Huang, but the concept of delivering incrementally goes back to Tom Gilb's work in 1988). This term refers to the minimum number of features that provide value to the customer. It is also called 'minimal viable product' (MVP). When used well, this means the customer can get an early look at the product with just the minimal features that will be built upon later in the project. Delivering something early without all the planned features can be a great way of testing the market's appetite for what you are delivering. No conversation about project scope can ignore the possibility of prioritising and delivering in small increments of value.

In Chapter 1, we talked about how to create a great project vision statement by asking questions. A great project sponsor can answer questions such as 'What purpose do you want this for?' and 'What will this give you?' This leads you to understanding what else a great project outcome will lead to, known as the project's 'higher intention'. This higher intention cannot be directly measured in terms of financial benefits, but is critical to understand, as many projects are simply enablers for bigger and better things.

A great project sponsor can take the project team on a journey to help them understand how what is 'in' (in terms of scope) will lead to the project's vision and higher intention, and how what is 'out' will be wasteful. Again, spending time on this higher intention may seem a bit up in the clouds and time wasting, but remember, everyone is motivated in different ways and the more ways the vision can be articulated, the better the project's scope will be.

Commitment

A pig and a chicken decide to go into business together and open a cafe. The chicken suggests they call the cafe *Bacon and Eggs*. The pig says 'that doesn't sound fair – you're only involved and I'm committed'.

Your stakeholder conversations around scope should only involve the 'pigs': the people who are truly committed to the project and stand to benefit the most from its success or lose the most from its failure. Of course, it's best not to call them pigs – even in a metaphorical sense. Review your stakeholder commitment chart from Chapter 3. Who do you need involved in scope conversations? And who do you NOT need? Be honest ...

Agile Planning and Estimating – MoSCoW

Through open and honest conversation with the right people, the scope is understood and the project's backlog is formed. It is now important to prioritise because, at the start of any project, the project scope in its entirety can look quite feasible. Before you have delved into the detail, it is easy to look at the backlog of high-level requirements (sometimes known as 'epics' or 'features') and say 'Yes, we can do this!'

The truth is that things on projects change, requirements become more complex or time-consuming than originally anticipated. Also, through changing business or market conditions, additional requirements could be added to the list. Agile practices encourage changing requirements and encourage us to be flexible and embrace this.

By prioritising from the start, you are sending a clear message – this is the order of priority in this project. If we run out of time/money/resources/energy, we will draw a line – everything above the line will get done, while everything below the line will not. It also helps to prioritise in what order the epics are broken down into more detailed requirements or 'stories'.

Remember, we only want to do 'just enough' and that means we only plan in more detail what we are going to do immediately next. If we are not tackling something for a bit longer (say a few weeks), let's focus on what we are doing first (say, next week).

This is why Agile planning uses the MoSCoW method: Must, Should, Could, Won't:

Must: these are the scope items that MUST be done. If they are not done, the project will fail. They are critical to the project outcome. If there is a chance that not all the Musts will done, the project should reconsider starting in the first place.

Should: these are the scope items that SHOULD be done. The project won't fail without them, but the benefits could be eroded as a result. Some people call them 'nice to haves' but I don't think that's the right language. The Shoulds form a critical part of your project scope and cannot be overlooked.

Could: these are the scope items that COULD be done, time and budget permitting. The project won't fail without them and they don't have as many benefits attached to them as the Shoulds, but they still have benefits – both financial and non-financial. However, we could get away without doing them and still be successful.

Won't: these are the things that we have discussed as specifically NOT doing. They start to form the out-of-scope conversations you have as part of your project set-up. This can serve as a great communication tool for people who enter the project late in the game and ask 'Why wasn't xxx considered?' Each item in Won't should have a brief statement as to why it has been included. This can save a lot of time and energy later in the project.

MoSCoW

Of course, this is not to say that items will not move from one category to another. As well as the concept of 'just enough', projects embracing Agility accept change as a part of the project. This flexibility means the project gets the very best outcome for now, not the best outcome that was relevant months ago. The project vision might change as a result of a change of sponsor, organisational direction or market conditions. More information may come to light on a specific scope item, changing its status. Engaging the right, committed stakeholders in the MoSCoW discussion ensures that what is 'in' and what is 'out' have been decided through collaboration and trust, and the project is off to a great start. The trust developed as part of this discussion means that later in the project, when these discussions might have to happen again due to changes, they will happen with that same level of trust and collaboration.

Use MoSCoW at the start of a project when planning scope, and ensure it is reviewed and updated regularly to keep up with changes that could influence the project.

Know Yourself

I learned a lot from Jacques about containing my project scope to ensure success and I believe one of the things that made him so successful was that he truly knew himself. He knew his skills, he knew his experience, he knew himself as a person. It was this self-knowledge or self-awareness that made it so easy for him to say yes or no to potential changes in his scope. He was an extremely self-assured person.

> "He who knows another is wise;
> he who knows himself is enlightened."
>
> Lao Tzu

Great PMs know what they want. They know themselves. This makes it easy for them to say yes or no to certain projects or work for particular organisations. It's no accident that they always end up with dream projects. They engineer this by knowing themselves so well that they always get the great gigs. They have most likely said no to some great-sounding projects along the way because they inherently knew those projects weren't right for them.

I encourage you to think about what it is you stand for, in the same way as you think about your project's scope. What is your vision? What is your Why? if you have not done the exercise in Chapter 1, I urge you to do it now, because knowing your Why is the same as knowing your project vision. The better you know it, the more you are able to clearly define what it is you are prepared to do and what it is you are not. This is the scope of your life. Your Identity.

The cool thing about your identity is that it is unique to you. As Oscar Wilde has been attributed as saying, "Be yourself; everyone else is taken". The even cooler thing is that you can write this yourself. It's completely up to you and no one else. People may have certain expectations or opinions of you, but at the end of the day those are just their thoughts, not yours. You have a blank canvas.

What do you want to be known for? What are the things that you want to do and achieve, that define who you are and lead to your Why? Just as project scope links to project vision, what you do must link to your Why, otherwise why bother? What is it that you will not do?

What are your Won'ts? It's worth spending some time thinking about this too. Not too much time, mind you, just enough to help you become clear on what you want to do and how it contributes to your vision.

What are Your Musts?

A few months ago, I got a friendly reminder text message that my next dental check-up was due. I made a note to book an appointment. It sat mid-way down my 'to do' list but was not given much attention. A few weeks later, I was eating some almonds and a tooth broke. As it turned out, this was the filling my dentist had put a watch on and recommended that at some point it would need to be replaced. Making a dental appointment suddenly went to the top of my 'to do' list: it went from being a Should to being a Must.

Sometimes the things we classify as Shoulds are really Musts, but we just don't see that yet. And the thing about Musts is that we always do them. Like critical project scope items, if we don't do them, failure ensues.

Possibility versus Necessity

There are two ways of thinking about the things that we need to do – possibility and necessity. Necessity-type language uses words such as 'must' and 'should': 'I really should go to the gym', 'I must call this person immediately'. The danger with necessity language is that it limits us and assigns negativity when things aren't done the way they 'should' be done. The answer is to use the language of possibility: 'I could go the gym', 'It would be great to call this person'. This opens up the unconscious mind to possibility.

It also ensures that our necessity language is reserved for the REAL necessities. The real Musts. It clears the mind and helps us to prioritise.

Imagine your 'to do' list without this thinking:

- Call Mother
- Clean kitchen
- Finish project plan before steering committee meeting
- Update project management plan with latest changes for approval
- Call project sponsor
- Schedule a project team meeting
- Check Facebook

The list goes on. What is really a Must? What is a Could? What might you get away without doing today? Or at all?

By applying the MoSCoW method to everything in your life, you give volition to your Musts and take the pressure off yourself for things that could be done later. And as with your Why, the only person who defines what is a Must, Should or Could is you. Perhaps except your mother, if you put off calling her for too long.

Your Values

By approaching your life and goals in a similar way to your project's Musts, Shoulds, Coulds and Won'ts, you can obtain great insight into what are known as your values. Understanding your values can be challenging, as many of us, when stating our values, state the values we aspire to as opposed to the ones we are living right now. Many a person has talked about how much they value honesty, transparency and health, but have clearly not demonstrated these. It is great to aspire and it is also great to know where you are right now. Like the commitment chart in Chapter 3, understanding that gap is key to getting to where you need to be.

When thinking about your values, it is important to understand that your values are not just internal to you, but are influenced by the external environment. For example, priorities and values can change when you experience a life event such as a death or natural disaster. Your external environment cannot be ignored.

Values Elicitation Exercise

Understanding your own personal values can go a long way to explaining why issues may exist between you and your team members. Or shed light on why you work so well with others. What is important to you? What are the things you simply 'Must' do? This is your critical personal project 'scope'. With the knowledge of your own personal Musts, Shoulds, Coulds and Won'ts and a clear idea of how your environment may be influencing you, think about the themes that are most important to you as an individual. It can be helpful to reflect on this and take some time to elicit your most important values. Your values could be anything – values include: integrity, achievement, success, creativity, being liked, humour and fun, personal fulfilment, respect etc.

If you want to truly understand yourself and get insight into how you interact with others, take some time to assess your own values. There are some great tools available online to help you with this and I highly recommend you do this as a personal exercise. Check out valuescentre.com for a free assessment. The key is to ensure you pick the values that are actually yours right NOW, as opposed to the ones you would like to have. What do you value at your very core? A mentor of mine once told me that if I was not sure what I valued, I could check out my credit card statement. What you spend money on is a good indicator of what is important to you. Are you living the values you want to be living? If you had to

96

prioritise them, which value would come first? Which would come second and so on? Are there any gaps? What do you need to do to fill these? This exercise will help you to work out your Musts: these are the things that you will always do, no matter what.

So now you know your Why AND are starting to get a clearer idea of the things you must do and the things you won't do. You understand your values and any gaps between what you aspire to and where you are now. Eliciting your values is not an easy exercise, especially if you have not done this in the past. Like anything else, it gets easier with practice. I encourage you to re-evaluate this on a regular basis. As with a project, things change and your ability to respond to change will ultimately determine your results.

> "It is not the strongest of the species that survives,
> nor the most intelligent that survives.
> It is the one that is most adaptable to change."

> Unknown (often attributed to Charles Darwin)

What This Means for You

Once you know your values, you know your Musts, as they reflect your values and align with your purpose. This helps greatly in determining what roles, what projects and what organisations are right for you. You will be one of the elite few who always seem to get the great projects with people wondering how you do it. Now you know!

Chapter Summary:

- Why understanding your scope clearly is so important.

- How to define scope so there is no doubt.

- Why knowing yourself is key to your success.

- How to re-examine your Why.

- Your values – why they are important and how to know what they are.

... Or The How ...

> "Slow down.
> Calm down.
> Don't worry.
> Don't hurry.
> Trust the process."
>
> Alexandra Stoddard

The project vision has now been created, key risks understood, stakeholders identified and scope confirmed. You are well on the way to project success. A lot of energy has been expended up until this point. Engaging stakeholders and getting them on board takes effort. Talking about what could go wrong and how to avoid it can challenge people emotionally. Confirming the most important scope can lead to conflict between stakeholders and team members. How can you bring all this together so the project hums along nicely?

The answer is: systems, processes and tools. While not the sexiest of all the things the Agile PM does, these will sustain you and ensure your project continues in a way that is consistent and visible. As with any job around the house, from moving to repairing to renovating, the right tools for the job are essential.

The energy that you, your team and your stakeholders have expended up to this point has been high, most likely in short but bright bursts – a type of creative energy. The energy that you need from now on is more of a slow burn, a type of energy that will sustain you over time.

Systems and processes sustain the project and keep it organised and on track. When these have been put in place properly, the Agile PM always knows what they need to do next and has a plan for responding to anything unexpected that might come up in the course of the project. Templates and processes are examples of tools that help the project team in planning and responding to change. They set the project up for success.

Dangers of Doing This too Early

This isn't just about the Agile value of valuing processes and tools less than individuals and interactions. This is about processes that promote sustainable development. The Agile principle states "the sponsors, developers and users should be able to maintain a constant pace indefinitely". Effective processes will enable this, the key word being 'enable'. Many project managers and stakeholders fall into the trap of defining templates, tools and processes too early in the project – before the vision is understood. While having organisation and order is extremely important to a project, enforcing order too early stifles creativity and prevents the vision from fully coming to life. Templates are only good once you have great content to go into them and they are used for the purpose of enabling, not driving. Trying to fill a gap just because you have to can prevent out-of-the-box thinking and silence thoughtful conversations.

So grab for a tool or process and avoid filling in a template too early in your change initiative. Later in this chapter I will share my change initiative checklist, which you can use as a guide to record key points from workshops about vision, risks, stakeholders and scope, while not interfering with the conversations and creation process.

The most important tool the Agile PM uses is the tool that brings to life the project's Why, Who, What and risks – in the format of a collaborative session with your stakeholders. The Agile PM focuses on conversation over documentation, collaboration over one-on-one interaction.

How to Use This Chapter

Until now, we have spoken about the concepts a great Agile PM needs to understand in order to run a great project or change initiative. A lot of Why and What. This chapter is a practical application of these concepts, as well as other essential tools and processes you can use – the How.

Perhaps you are already doing some of these processes and can pick up some new ideas, or perhaps these are brand new. These processes are intended to ensure you have all the supporting tools you need in order to bring the Agile PM's concepts to life and apply them practically.

How to Identify the MOST Important Thing

While the vision and scope may be understood, it's also important to understand from the sponsor what the MOST important thing is to them.

- Is it getting every scope item done?

- Is it finishing within a set budget?

- Is it finishing by a certain time?

While these three parameters are important, this 'iron triangle' is not the only definition of success. Other things to consider are:

- How much money are you willing to spend to ensure we have a quality product?

- To what extent do we need to keep our stakeholders satisfied? Which stakeholders in particular?

- How critical are financial benefits? Or are all benefits non-financial?

- How hard are we willing to push the team? What does their work/life balance look like?

- How important is customer satisfaction?

How many projects have you heard of that have delivered all or most of their scope on time, on budget, but have still been failures? Failure can happen for a number of reasons:

- What you delivered is not being used by the customer as intended (or at all)

- The benefits identified have not been realised

- The quality has ended up being poor, rendering the end result unusable

- The end result is not easily understood by key stakeholders and has not been used

- The end result does not delight key stakeholders

... The list goes on. Research has found that the biggest reason for project failure is people-related (McKinsey, 2012). So even sticking to time, cost and scope parameters can put your project at risk. People fit into this and cannot be forgotten. The question is, how?

The purpose of having systems and processes to sustain your project is so key decisions can be communicated easily and effortlessly, and the project vision is delivered without compromise. Key messages reach the right people and the project continues to deliver successfully AND is perceived as delivering successfully.

This perception is critical. A project can be delivering well, hitting its milestones and generally being successful, but if key messages are not being delivered to the right people, the PERCEPTION will be (or could be) that the project is not doing well. Conversely, a project could be failing at every turn, but if the right stakeholders are involved and understand the situation, the perception will still be positive. Strange, right?

By now you should be convinced that having great systems is a necessity and the timing is so important. Let's talk about some of these tools now.

How did You Get Here? Rapid Planning

Throughout the first few chapters, we have spoken about the importance of collaboration and transparency, and we have touched on different ways of eliciting the project's outcome, scope, risks and stakeholders. A great Agile PM uses a number of different tools to ensure stakeholders are identified and engaged, and scope is understood and communicated.

By far the best technique I have learned is the concept of rapid planning. Rapid planning has been known by many names by many people and Rob Thomsett is known for his ability to achieve great results from his rapid planning workshops (or RAPs). Fundamentally it involves getting into a room together everyone who is critical to the success of the project and planning out the project at a high level.

The focus of the workshop is very much the Why and the What. The best order in which to talk things through is based on a combination of how people naturally think, values levels and the Disney Creativity Strategy (developed by Robert Dilts). As we saw in Chapter 3, in any group of people there are the people who are motivated by 'towards' language and those who are motivated by 'away' language. You may want to generalise and call them the optimists and the pessimists. The most important thing is to have a mix of people who can contribute to a robust discussion that draws out the vision, risks, people and scope. And I do mean robust. Nodding heads are fine, but a great discussion involves some disagreement.

Rapid Planning Workshop Steps

1. **The project outcome or vision** – this is when the sponsor and key team members communicate to the room what is important for them to achieve from this project. It is important at this point to only use positive language and talk about possibilities – what this outcome will mean to the business, to the organisation, to the world. The project sponsor then has to choose the most important thing – what is the one thing we are aiming for? If you have a great sponsor, they will already have a great statement in mind that the room can add to using 'Wouldn't it be great if …?' and 'Yes and …' statements. The objective of this part of the workshop is to finalise (or come close to finalising) the project vision statement. This is then written up somewhere visible for everyone to see and refer back to. Prework: spending time with the sponsor and key members of the team beforehand will ensure this goes as smoothly as possible. Any opportunity to ensure that the sponsor fully understands the Why of their project is time well spent.

2. **Hopes and fears** – according to the Disney Creativity Strategy, when building a dream always start with the positive (known as the 'dreamer') and do not bring in the negative until the dream is fully understood. It is also important not to put off talking about what could go wrong for too long (the 'realist' and the 'critic'). This part of the workshop is all about brainstorming both – the dream and the things that could go wrong – and is a great opportunity for the Agile PM to learn how their stakeholders think. With the project vision fully visible in the room, take two pieces of butchers paper (and some spares) and get everyone to write on sticky notes their 'hopes' for the project and their 'fears' for the project. I recommend doing each consecutively so everyone can focus on each fully. Encourage participants to keep input to a high level, based on the project's vision. Use the sticky notes as a basis for a deep discussion about the key things the team must look out for that could potentially derail the project. Encourage questions that don't need to be answered straight away. This exercise gives you not only benefits and risks, but also dependencies and actions to take away from the workshop. Prework: ensure when selecting stakeholders for the workshop that you have a good balance of people who will contribute equally to hopes and fears.

3. **Stakeholders** – this is all about the Who. Who is going to ensure this project is successful? Who is so critical to its success that if they left the project suddenly, it would grind to a halt? All these people should be in the room if your preparation has been good, but who else, based on our project vision, hopes and fears, needs to be involved? What is their role? How will they support the project? Who will benefit most from this, the sponsor or someone else? Who is critical in delivering the project? Who is critical in

supporting the project once it is in? And who is critical in ensuring the project benefits are realised? The word 'critical' comes up a lot – because at this point we are only talking about the people who ARE critical. Anyone else helping, or mildly assisting, can be talked about later.

4. **Forcefield analysis** – this is a decision-making framework developed by Kurt Lewin (1943). It is a great opportunity to look at the critical stakeholders and do a high-level analysis of what benefits they are going to 'win' and also what they might 'lose'. According to Newton's laws, for every action there is an equal and opposite force. So there may be a stakeholder that stands to 'win' by increasing revenue for their business unit (and ultimately the organisation); however, the equal and opposite force (which could get brushed over in the excitement) is the additional responsibility and pressure on this business unit's staff. While they may all be excited about this change, it's still a 'loss' because something has to change. And this change needs to be managed. Prework: work with your project sponsor to identify the people who need to be in the room – your critical stakeholders. Use the hierarchy of ideas to brainstorm 'Who else?' to ensure that you not only have the right people in the room to have the conversation, but you also have your draft list of stakeholders prior to this exercise.

5. **Scope** – now that we know the Why and the Who and what could go wrong, the room is in a good position to talk about the What. What are the key, tangible outputs the team must deliver in order to achieve the project vision? What is the minimum we can get away with? What are some other great things that could be left for another project? What are we prepared to do and what are we NOT prepared to do? This part of the workshop is about

identifying the project's unique identity and values. What do we stand for? Who are we? I love using the metaphor about the jar that needs to be filled with rocks, pebbles, sand and water. In order to get everything in, you must start with the biggest element: the rocks. This exercise is all about identifying those big rocks first. Prework: it's great if some thinking has been done around this and brought into the room, and it's also okay if the room is fresh and starting from scratch. Wherever the team is, they are in the right place for them.

6. **Key milestones and high-level approach** – what are some key dates we need to hit? How might we approach these in terms of people and processes? What governance do we need to have in place? This is an excellent chance to cover the administrative side without taking away from the important thinking done earlier in the workshop. Prework: if any 'hard dates' are known, especially other pieces of work that depend on outputs from the project, have them ready to contribute to this exercise. They could be regulatory, but may also be based on expectations of customers from marketing or other channels of the business.

7. **Next steps** – this workshop does not cover everything that needs to be done in order to fully plan the project. There are going to be some key next steps to plan in more detail and to act on any risks that may have been identified. Ensure these are clearly identified and handed to the people best placed to action them.

RAPID PLANNING WORKSHOP STEPS

VISION

HOPES + FEARS

NEXT STEPS

RAPID PLANNING

MILESTONES

STAKEHOLDERS

SCOPE

FORCEFIELD ANALYSIS

Beyond Rapid Planning – collaboration in action

In Chapter 2, we talked about the dangers of planning for risk and then not following through. Rapid planning can be a similar panacea. Without continuing the open, collaborative conversations from the rapid planning session, there is a risk that the planning will not be converted into resourceful action. Here are some techniques for keeping the collaborative approach going and the project progressing as planned. In summary, they follow a simple approach I have developed.

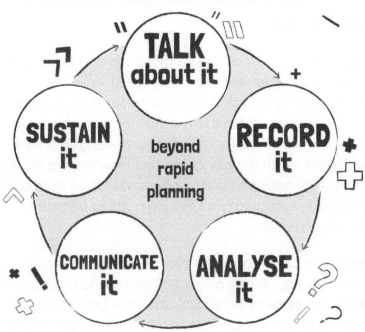

T.R.A.C.S.: COLLABORATION IN ACTION

TALK about it

RECORD it

ANALYSE it

COMMUNICATE it

SUSTAIN it

beyond rapid planning

They also happen to form a handy acronym – TRACS:

Talk about it

Record it

Analyse it

Communicate it

Sustain it

Let's see how we can apply TRACS to key processes throughout the project so that the collaboration and trust developed in rapid planning can continue.

Risk Management

Talk about it: while risk and issue meetings can be dreaded, they need to happen regularly. The great Agile PM uses them as an opportunity to catch up with the team and understand some of their concerns in more detail than can be covered in the daily stand-up. The focus in these meetings is on the conversation. What is really going on? How are we managing the things that could go wrong or could stop us from doing well? Monitoring regularly is key and holding people to account is essential.

Record it: the best tool is a simple risk and issues matrix. The simpler the better. Many project offices like to have lots of columns, but those columns are valuable only if they are actively used. If the team is not up to talking about residual risk (or they don't know what it is), leave it out. Simply identify the risk, the actions that need to happen, the owner and the next check-in.

Analyse it: what poses a serious threat? Classify risks as high, medium or low, and ensure all have owners, especially the ones that are 'high'. What action plans do we need to have in place?

Communicate it: action plans are all very well, but people will continue to worry about a risk unless they know something is being done about it. Although this may seem a bit negative, risks classified as 'high' should be communicated widely. The sooner people are aware of problems AND what is being done to solve them, the better.

Sustain it: one risk meeting a year is simply not enough. Commit to meeting regularly and keep this going.

Stakeholder Management

While risk management can be systemised fairly easily, stakeholder management is a more complicated beast. However, by applying the TRACS approach, it can be made simpler.

Talk about it: firstly, have the conversation. Who are the key stakeholders? What are the key messages that need to be communicated? How often? Is their level of commitment where you need it to be?

Record it: again, keep it simple. Create a stakeholder matrix that identifies the key stakeholders, their wants and needs, key messages and any gaps in commitment (see the commitment chart from Chapter 3).

Analyse it: what's changed? What do we need to focus on most? What actions do we need to take immediately? Who needs to do what and when?

Communicate it: let your stakeholders know what's happening. Let them know the key messages relevant to them via their preferred learning style (see Chapter 3).

Sustain it: keep it going by committing to regularly updating your stakeholder matrix and communications plan.

Scope Management

The same can be done with scope management. This approach ensures your scope is well managed with changes that are well understood, recorded and communicated. As

Peter Taylor says in *The Lazy Project Manager* (2011): "manage the creep".

Talk about it: first, as always, have the conversation. How are we going with delivering the required scope? Are there any potential changes? If so, what is the purpose of this change? What are the risks? Who needs to be involved in deciding if this is a good thing for the project?

Record it: record the key points in a (simple) change register.

Analyse it: what are the impacts of this change? Consider effects on timing, costs and quality. Benefits must also be considered. What might be a tiny change could have a far-reaching impact on the benefits that will be achieved – both financial and non-financial. What are our options? Who needs to be informed?

Communicate it: communicate the outcomes of your analysis to the stakeholders involved – get their input and feedback, ensuring the right people are involved in the decision-making process. Send out final analyses and outcomes of decision-making to all involved stakeholders. Remember that different people need to be communicated to in different ways. A 'hi everyone' email will not cut the mustard, especially if the change has a material impact on the recipients.

Sustain it: sustain the process by checking in with your stakeholders. Have there been any unintended outcomes of the change? Are they still happy with the decision? Commit to regularly checking in, so that potential changes can be captured as early as possible.

Team Management and Engagement

Often overlooked, keeping the team engaged and excited about the project can be challenging but nowhere near impossible. Sometimes your project is up against almost impossible odds and these situations lend themselves to late nights, early mornings and a poor work/life balance. Over time, this can lead to lower engagement and poor performance.

Talk about it: as always, start with the conversation. How is the team feeling? Knowledge workers are affected severely by setbacks such as bureaucratic requirements, technical dependencies and missed opportunities. Consider a budget for team events – pizza, lunches, morning teas etc – as a way of recognising their efforts. A happy team is more productive and future-focused. An unhappy team dwells on past events and not on the future success of the project. A great Agile PM keeps the team future-focused wherever possible.

Record it: keep track of the team's engagement. While a survey may be tempting, consider Agile tools such as a 'mood meter' where the team members place their avatars against a thermometer image to show where they are in terms of happiness and engagement. It's a bit of fun, but drives some serious conversations if people are towards the bottom of the thermometer for too long.

Analyse it: which people or teams have been feeling the pinch for a while? How long has this gone on? What are some of the contributing factors? What can be done about it? A great Agile PM protects their team from outside forces that distract them from doing great work.

Communicate it: a simple 'thank you' goes a long way. Consider team-specific recognition programs to encourage people to actively be grateful for hard work and extra effort. A great Agile PM regularly updates their stakeholders on the hard work being done by the team in the form of regular newsletters or team updates.

Sustain it: commit to checking in with the team regularly using tools such as the thermometer or group/individual check-ins. A recent *Harvard Business Review* report on employee engagement found that just 24% of respondents could say most of their employees were highly engaged (*Harvard Business Review* 'Analytics Report', September 2013).

I have put together a business initiative checklist for you to use these concepts in more detail. Go to www.theAgileprojectmanager.com.au/coolstuff.

Individuals and Interactions over Processes and Tools

I love this part of the *Agile Manifesto*. I know it's a strange place to bring this up, right in the middle of a chapter on systems and processes, but your regular interactions are an important tool in a project. The tools outlined above are essential to success AND the way they are executed is critical – it is vital to focus on people, with processes and tools simply supporting those interactions.

Our interactions CAN be systemised. Planning in regular team meetings, one-on-one catch-ups and planning sessions well in advance give the team the ability to plan other activities around those. Then team members know when they can focus on their work and when they are needed to be involved in activities that take them away from their individual work. It may sound strange, but planning actually enables more

Agility because it's clear when the opportunities are to think, work and collaborate.

Reporting

Reporting is central to the stakeholder management undertaken by a great Agile PM because it is a great communication tool and a fabulous opportunity to reach out to stakeholders who may not be 'inside the tent' yet. The flexibility of Agile reporting options provides a number of different tools to get your point across. Visuals are a must – photos of the team doing planning or the visual management board are a great way of humanising the project team and making them real for stakeholders. Sending photos of the outcomes of retrospectives is an efficient way to share outputs without spending hours writing minutes or preparing a PowerPoint pack.

Another useful reporting tool is the burn-down chart or the burn-up chart – where progress over time, whether it be progress towards completion or progress towards reducing issues, is clearly illustrated. Jason Fox in his book *The Game Changer* states that people love seeing visible progress and it is highly motivating to see achievements clearly. A team I once coached would break out into applause when a task made its way across the Kanban board. What positive reinforcement!

Now, Let's Talk about You

In order for the Agile PM to succeed at work, great systems are needed at home too. What sustains you? What regular routines energise you and keep you motivated to work? There are thousands of books out there on time management, but what many of them don't say is that there is no 'one size fits all' to self-management. The good news is that by using Agile principles, developing systems to sustain you personally is within your reach, because the great Agile PM has not only a clear project vision, but also a clear personal vision. They know exactly where they are going. They know their Why. And when you know your Why, knowing how you can achieve that becomes a lot easier. For example, many people who have the goal of running a marathon but no clear Why or purpose for running it will fail. Those with a clear purpose will run barefoot over broken glass to achieve it. So, however you choose to sustain yourself, it must be in line with that Why.

Many time-management systems say 'don't check email in the morning'. The *Harvard Business Review* published a great article called 'Manage Your Energy, not Your Time' (October 2007) that talks about the importance of knowing when you are at your best. For example, I have more energy in the morning than I do later in the afternoon. So for me, the morning is about creative endeavours such as writing or brainstorming new ideas. My afternoons are for administrative tasks such as banking and replying to emails. One of my colleagues, on the other hand, focuses on administrative tasks in the morning, such as emails and spreadsheets, but at 4 pm her eyes light up and she's ready to do some serious thinking and creating. There is no one size fits all. When are you at your best? What tasks suit you best at what times? Don't fight nature – go with the flow and use your energy well. Use TRACS to work out how you can become even better at spending your time wisely.

Talk about it: ask your friends and co-workers – when do they think you are at your best? Ask yourself – when do things just seem to flow?

Record it: consider keeping a record of when things really work for you (and when they don't). Note the times and look for trends.

Analyse it: what are some consistent patterns? You may notice that your focus just isn't there at an 8 am meeting, but at 5 pm you are full of beans. You may notice that morning exercise sets you up for a great day or you are brilliant at the gym in the evening.

Communicate it: once you know when you are at your best, let others know. This does not mean declining that 8 am meeting, but it may mean talking with your co-workers and friends about timings for events that work better for you. Armed with that knowledge, they are better equipped to work in with your preferred timings. They will probably appreciate your candour.

Sustain it: commit to checking in on what is working for you and what isn't in terms of activities throughout your day. Checking in regularly ensures you are always working (and playing) at your very best.

The great Agile PM has great personal routines and habits that sustain them over time. They are healthy, happy and balanced. As you know, there is no 'one size fits all' approach – what makes you happy and healthy is individual to you. Take some time to ensure you are sustaining yourself in the very best way that sets you up for personal and professional success.

Chapter Summary:

- Systems and processes sustain change.
- They can be as simple as TRACS:
  - Talk about it
  - Record it
  - Analyse it
  - Communicate it
  - Sustain it
- Consider people's values when collaborating on a project.
- Everything can be systemised and sustainability is key.

... Or Be Open to Opportunities ...

I once had a project sponsor encourage our group of project managers to 'be bold! Think of other opportunities! What else can we do to deliver "amazing" to our customers?' I think this is a fabulous idea. The only problem with this situation was that it was after 6 pm at the tail end of a long program meeting where the message throughout was 'there's no more money, we need to do what we can with what we have'. Downcast faces and looks of resignation prevailed. How can we 'be bold' when we are looking down the barrel of the possibility of not finishing our projects at all?

While that situation did not lend itself to an opportunity for excellence, the sponsor's (perhaps badly timed) words were absolutely true. No matter what the situation – dire or brilliant – the great Agile PM is always on the lookout for opportunities to be excellent, both personally and professionally.

"Excellence is not a skill. It is an attitude."

Ralph Marston

While I sympathise with the 'downtrodden PM' who works 12 hours a day just to deliver their project, the Agile PM must think differently and not fall into this mindset. The Agile PM must have an attitude of excellence and it must be part of everything they do.

At a recent event I attended, Julia Gillard, Australia's first female prime minister, was asked if there was anything she would do differently if she could have her time as prime minister again. She replied that one of the things she did as much as she could in her time as prime minister was to take time out to "just think". But in a busy world (and I can't begin to imagine how busy her world was compared to the average project manager's), there is always an email or phone call to answer, or something else that requires attention. Even with all that going on, Julia Gillard still made the time to think. If she could have her time again, she said she would make even more thinking time. Firstly, I was impressed that she made time to think – how did she make the time? And even more impressed with the value she placed on this time.

It is just as important for the Agile PM to take the time to reflect as it is for the person sharing our initials with the responsibilities of a nation, or any person with responsibility for that matter. Without taking the time out to think ahead, poor decisions get made in the present that threaten future success. Sometimes just a few minutes of thinking clearly can save hours, days, weeks of wasted effort down the track. Taking the time to think is not a luxury, but an absolute must. While this chapter is called 'Opportunities for Excellence' and appears later in the book, do not mistake it for an optional extra. It is an absolute Must.

Let's go back to the downtrodden PM who works 12 hours a day and only just manages to deliver their project. I have coached many PMs and come across this regularly. Indeed, I have been that PM, still in the office at 8 pm putting together a pack, writing an email communication or balancing my finances, and still only just staying ahead. So how do we move from being THAT PM to being the Agile PM who has bandwidth to look out for opportunities to 'be bold' and be excellent?

Why be Excellent?

This is an opportunity for the Agile PM to stand out and it could be the single most important answer to your question – 'How come that guy gets all the best gigs?' You see, it's not enough to deliver a project as requested. Delivering a project as required is hard, but not impossible. Delivering a project with excellence is how a great PM is distinguished from a good one.

Of course, you may just get lucky and your stakeholders love you. This means they forgive and forget any glaring errors you make. Unfortunately, this alone is not enough. Who is to say your stakeholders on your next project will be just as willing to overlook your gaffes?

Embodying a culture of excellence in everything you do will not only mean your projects are delivered with exceptional results, but you will continue to get great projects to run in the future.

A culture of excellence begins with the mindset that there is an abundance of opportunities out there just waiting to be found. Simply believing this is the first and most vital step.

I think of this concept of opportunities as not so much opportunities to 'be bold' but opportunities to make my project 'even better'. It could be:

- an opportunity to save money by streamlining some activities
- an opportunity to leverage work with another project or business unit

- an opportunity to take on new scope that could lead to more business benefits
- an opportunity to reach out to a new stakeholder for additional support and help
- a possibility that was identified earlier being realised

This can be challenging when your back is to the wall and your financial forecasts are due by the close of business.

Or IS this challenging? What if it wasn't?

Your Own Backlog

As we spoke about in Chapter 4 (Know your Scope), an Agile project generally includes what's known as a backlog – a list of project requirements (sometimes called stories) that are prioritised by the product owner/business representative and team. Because many Agile projects are time-bound or budget-bound, they are given a finite period to complete work. This means that the lever you work with is scope. If a scope item is added, another one should generally be taken away. If something is more complex than initially thought, its benefit is reassessed along with the effort and the story is either re/de-prioritised or another story removed from the backlog.

I think of it as a jug you fill with water: once the jug is full, it will overflow, so if you want to put more water into the jug, you must empty some water out of the jug first. I believe that a great Agile PM has their own backlog. Time is our finite resource – there are only so many hours in the day and there are always more scope items than there is time. So we must prioritise and accept that not everything will get done.

MANAGING BACKLOG (FACT: there's only so
much you can take on at the one time – really, there is.)

So how does the Agile PM make time to "just think" as Julia Gillard recommends, as well as dealing with the competing demands of a project?

As we talked about in the previous chapter, the secret is to identify the times of the day that you are at your best using our TRACS system: Talk about it, Record it, Analyse it, Communicate it, Sustain it. Author Dr Wayne Dyer claims his best writing time starts at about 3 am (!), while other writers swear that getting up at 5 am works for them. For you, it could be the afternoon. When do you get your best ideas? When is it best to simply get through your emails? When are you most comfortable making those difficult phone calls?

And as no Agile PM is an island, it can't just be about you, so when are your critical stakeholders most available and willing to talk to you? Here is where compromises must be made. If one of your most critical stakeholders is a morning person and bouncing around the office at 7 am while you're still pressing the snooze button, it may be worth getting in extra early one day a week to have that important conversation.

For me, my most creative thinking time is first thing in the morning. If I can carve out an hour – whether it be at home, on my commute, alone at my desk or hiding out in a meeting room – first thing in the morning, then the rest of my day flows. Sometimes I choose instead to spend that time addressing emails and getting stuck into my day early and although this feels more productive, in the long term I suffer from missing out on that valuable thinking time.

Tony Robbins insists that we should have an "hour of power" every day dedicated to long-term improvement – whether it be listening to an educational podcast or power walking. Some time during that hour is dedicated to being grateful for what you have and for what you want to have but haven't achieved yet. This is what he calls your "Musts" – the things that simply MUST be done and will never be de-prioritised.

As we talked about in Chapter 4, all scope items need to be categorised as Musts, Shoulds, Coulds or Won'ts. What are yours? What are they REALLY? And of course, just as a great Agile PM ensures the backlog is not overflowing, leading to disappointment in their project, they apply the same thinking to their personal success. They always have some room in their personal backlog for something more if it comes up. AND within that backlog, time to "just think" has been scheduled.

The Importance of Quadrant II

Still too much to do to make time to think? Think of the consequences of NOT making this time! Constantly being stuck, behind and frustrated. I found it difficult at first to stick to my promise to myself to have thinking time, so an interim step that I took was to adopt Stephen Covey's four-quadrant system, as outlined in *The Seven Habits of Highly Effective People*:

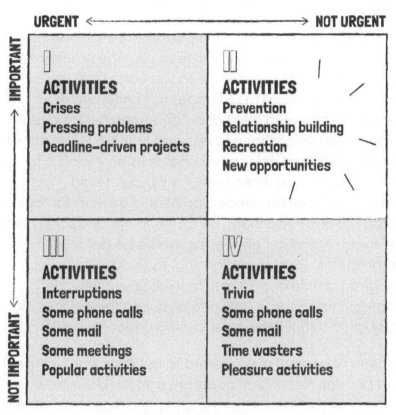

URGENT ⟵----------⟶ NOT URGENT

IMPORTANT

I

ACTIVITIES
Crises
Pressing problems
Deadline–driven projects

II

ACTIVITIES
Prevention
Relationship building
Recreation
New opportunities

III

ACTIVITIES
Interruptions
Some phone calls
Some mail
Some meetings
Popular activities

IV

ACTIVITIES
Trivia
Some phone calls
Some mail
Time wasters
Pleasure activities

NOT IMPORTANT

Ref: *The 7 Habits of Highly Effective People*
Stephen Covey (2004)

Quadrant I is where everyone is at times – Urgent and Important. This often involves working against the clock to submit something by a critical deadline. There is no getting out of this quadrant once in it – the work simply must be done. Anything else becomes a lower priority.

There will always be things that appear in Quadrant I, but this quadrant can be minimised by ensuring Quadrant II is managed well – these are the Important but Not Urgent tasks. They must be done, but don't have deadlines too soon. I believe thinking time exists in Quadrant II, a time to consider new opportunities. If it's not done here, it's not done.

Quadrant III is Urgent and Not Important – things that must be done right now but are of no value to you. The problem is that they are normally of great value to someone else. The expression 'your failure to plan does not constitute my emergency' comes to mind and can sometimes be useful, but mostly you simply have to respond to these incidents with as much grace and calm as you can muster. A classic for me was a few years ago when one of my project leads "just remembered" that he needed additional devices for testing but had not arranged them. He came to me and said I had to order them urgently or else testing would be delayed. I was disappointed in his lack of planning, especially as he had been given ample opportunity to think about this, but ultimately I made some calls and acquired the devices as quickly as I could (all the while cursing under my breath …).

Quadrant IV is sometimes referred to as 'Xbox time' – this is the Not Important, Not Urgent quadrant and this downtime can be critical to your success in the other quadrants. We all need time to chill out, watch some TV, go to a movie, go out to dinner etc. The key to success in this quadrant is that while you are in it, ENJOY IT! It can be easy to feel guilty for spending time here when there is other stuff to do. While writing this book, I would sometimes find myself feeling guilty for relaxing rather than writing, but often my best ideas came when I was taking time to chill out, guilt free. Of course, if the Quadrant II tasks are piling up and threatening to become Quadrant I, limiting your time in Quadrant IV is recommended.

Think about everything on your 'to do' list. Are you spending too much time in Quadrant I? How can you spend more time in Quadrant II? This book was in my Quadrant II for most of the time I was writing it, but started to become Quadrant I as my deadline drew closer.

Forest versus Trees and Strategy

The great thing about truly Agile teams is they contain self-managing, highly motivated individuals. This gives the Agile PM more time to be looking outwards, rather than managing inwards. This is great news, as this is where your focus needs to be. Of the 70% of change programs that fail or "are challenged" according to research conducted by McKinsey, the majority of the challenges faced are due to people. The great Agile PM is not only managing their stakeholders to a high standard as outlined in Chapter 3, they are also engaging with those people to explore possible futures, depending on the outcome of events.

Many PMs get caught out by 'failing to see the forest for the trees'. An Agile PM with an attitude of excellence focuses on both and takes time out to look at the bigger picture. You see, markets change constantly; new products are being produced by organisations at a faster rate than ever. The need to look at the big picture is becoming more urgent. How to do this? If you have chosen great stakeholders to be actively engaged in the project, use their experience and knowledge to talk not just about the day-to-day of the project, but also about their thoughts on the future. What do they think could happen next? How would we handle that?

A great tool to use is what is known as a 'pre-mortem'. The *Harvard Business Review* described this in the September 2007 issue and I have used it a number of times with success. It is a role play that pretends we are in the future and the project has failed. We sit down and analyse what went wrong. It's a great way of identifying risks that have not been considered before and taking time out to think of the worst possible outcome. More importantly, it's a great way of identifying potential opportunities. In fact, one of my teams insisted on doing the pre-mortem while pretending that everything had been a complete success: we sat together and workshopped all the reasons that it had gone so well. While I'm all for discovering the risks earlier, I found this exercise in identifying opportunities much more enlightening. What it also did was future-paced the project team. Imagine a room full of people imagining a positive outcome – this made the project vision even more real and gave everyone a taste of success.

Taking time out to consider the bigger picture is the equivalent of a sea captain looking up from their compass and taking in the wide expanse of ocean ahead of them. Looking ahead and anticipating problems and opportunities are critical to achieving excellent results.

Gold Plating

This is otherwise known as 'project stakeholders and sponsors behaving badly, resulting in the need for difficult conversations ...'.

Sometimes 'gold plating' comes disguised as an opportunity to 'be bold'. The astute Agile PM can easily identify the difference between these two. Gold plating is adding additional functionality or scope not originally agreed on and that does not add value to the overall outcome, so that the project would have been successful without it. Gold plating also introduces additional risk. An opportunity to be bold is something that was not previously thought of, but now that it has been, it will add significant value to the outcome. In fact, the overall outcome may not be achieved (or could be significantly eroded) without it.

Sometimes gold plating comes from a project sponsor 'behaving badly'. But at the end of the day, if the sponsor wants their 'great idea' in, they need to be open to the idea of something else coming out, or more funding and/or time being allocated to accommodate it. The Agile PM is comfortable with these uncomfortable conversations, which normally start with 'Sure, this additional scope could be included and it would cost $x or mean other scope (possibly of higher benefit) has to be removed – it's your call as the sponsor, I'm just highlighting it so you can make the best decision'. Or even more pointedly: 'That sounds like a great idea, I'm just confused about how it adds value or contributes to the project vision'.

Do you find yourself unable to have these uncomfortable conversations? Why is that? I'm always surprised at how many PMs cannot have these conversations and then wonder why their project scope is out of control. These conversations are critical in ensuring you are doing the right thing and they also guarantee that the right opportunity can be taken advantage of and acted on in a way that benefits the project. The wrong 'opportunity' can be quickly identified, discussed and discarded.

Benefits Realisation – start now

In search of excellence, the great Agile PM and their team demonstrate benefits (both financial and non-financial) as early as possible by working with the sponsor to prioritise scope or 'stories' of high business value. Demonstrating value early reinforces the vision and keeps stakeholders engaged and interested.

Conversely, the great Agile PM does not wait until the project goes live for someone else to measure benefits. You see, a project may look good on paper – be relatively low cost to execute, for example – but there could be hidden costs post go-live from support teams in the business or technology. Highlighting these costs early is critical, as there is no point in implementing a change that could end up ultimately costing the organisation more money than it saves, especially when the end goal or vision was to make or save money.

Note: the danger of this course of action is that you may demonstrate so much value so early that the sponsor may choose to finish the project earlier, before you have delivered everything. This is actually okay. Stopping a project and choosing to invest in something else because so much value has been delivered shows project and organisational maturity, and true Agility.

Expect the Best, Plan for the Worst

Balancing anticipating opportunities with managing risks almost seems like a paradox, but they can both be done well. It's a matter of balancing vision with what could go wrong. When planning the vision, expect the very best outcome. This engages people and opens up opportunities for creativity and a successful project mindset. The importance of this successful project mindset cannot be underestimated: the Agile PM not only sets the project up for success but also truly believes the project can be successful, even in the darkest hours when things are not looking as good as they could be. This belief, and the ability to convey it to your team, could be the difference between success and failure, between a good project and a great project.

"You must find a place inside yourself
where nothing is impossible."

Deepak Chopra

When planning around risks, imagine the worst-case scenario and have a plan in place for it. I highly recommend the pre-mortem approach described earlier in this chapter: I have seen both the 'everything failed' and 'everything went very well' approaches work equally successfully. If your team is balanced, it may appreciate both approaches so that everyone can contribute. Then confidently continue to deliver a great project, using the risk management process outlined in Chapter 5 to keep the project on track.

A Learning Mindset

The great Agile PM is always looking for ways to improve. This mindset is critical to success. A kung fu master once told me "you never reach perfection – even the most experienced black belt is still learning". Celebrate victories and at the same time always be on the lookout for how to improve. A great Agile PM is always open to learning new things. Don't close yourself to learning just because you are smart or have been around a while.

"If you're not green and growing, you're ripe and rotting."

Tony Robbins

Remember when we talked about the importance of asking Why? Adopt an attitude of child-like wonder and curiosity with anything unfamiliar. This ensures that your unconscious mind is open and ready to receive new information. Close your mind and you close opportunities for learning something that could make an amazing difference to you.

Yes, sometimes you are right and the other person is wrong. But what harm does it do to listen to their point of view anyway? The ability to do this without puffing out your IQ requires emotional intelligence (EQ), because being righteously indignant is so much easier. According to Daniel Goleman, author of *Emotional Intelligence*, EQ could well be much more important than IQ when it comes to professional and personal success. The great news is that we can all develop our EQ. The best way to develop your EQ is to take on an attitude of continuous learning, an attitude of being open to new things.

> "When given the choice between being right or being kind, choose kind, and you'll always be right."
>
> Dr Wayne Dyer

Key Learning Points

- Always be open to opportunities

- Make time to think

- Aim for excellence. Always!

- Manage your time. Focus on Quadrant II

- Expect the best, plan for the worst

- Never stop learning

CHAPTER SEVEN

... Or Be Focused and Flexible ...

At the start of any project or change initiative, you set a clear vision, a purpose for doing whatever it is that you are doing. From a complex technology change to a wedding to a house move, it is so important to understand what that purpose is and what success looks like.

Now, to stay the course. Throughout a project, throughout life, things change. Challenges arise that were either predicted through great risk brainstorming or else completely out of left field. Opportunities arise to change direction and take advantage of something not anticipated. How you deal with these in the context of your purpose determines your success.

If you have really thought through what success looks like, any challenge simply means adjusting your metaphorical sails and staying true to the ultimate direction you have set. I once had a project sponsor say "We are in the middle of the Pacific Ocean and we want to get to Australia – let's head west and adjust our course as we get closer. By then we will be clearer about where exactly in Australia we want to land".

I love this because it means that your purpose can be as broad or specific as you like. It can be broad so that it allows you to set off in a direction and then adjust, or it can be specific so that all the steps are known early. Some projects or changes have a specific outcome, others do not. Some projects evolve as they go along. As long as everyone understands this and broadly agrees, we are all good.

Staying true to purpose has another hidden advantage. It helps so much in deciding what is in and what is out. Having a clear purpose makes these decisions easier.

The great thing about Agile projects is the outcome doesn't need to be specifically identified in huge amounts of detail. A clear project vision that depends on a highly skilled team to bring it to life is the best start. As the project continues, there may be moments when the team is not sure where to go. The vision is the lighthouse, reminding them of their purpose and at the same time giving them flexibility on their course of action to get there.

Changing the Project Vision

The other great thing about Agile projects is that the work is done iteratively, with chunks of value being added all along the way. It means that at any time, if an opportunity arises from either external market forces or internal organisational change, the project can pivot and set course in a new direction. The vision could even change completely. Of course that means some work may not be needed anymore, but that's okay. The key here is understanding why the vision has changed and ensuring the team is on board to move in the new direction.

Staying True to YOUR Purpose

Throughout their career, the Agile PM will have many opportunities to implement change. Some of these opportunities will have clear, well thought-out purposes with great people. And others will not. Some will present challenges that no one should have to deal with. Others will present challenges that will be risen to and overcome. And every situation will be different for every person.

Knowing YOUR purpose, your vision, about what success looks like for you will determine your response to situations that arise, whether unexpected or anticipated.

As with a project where an issue arises and decisions need to be made about direction and problem-solving, the Agile PM needs to be ready to respond in a way that is true to their purpose. Your purpose might be to become the go-to Agile PM for everything to do with credit risk in banking. It might be your digital expertise. It might be your stakeholder management reputation. What will all of that give you? What is YOUR purpose? Knowing this makes it easy and effortless to respond to issues.

It also makes it easier to decide what to do on a day-to-day basis. It helps with your Musts. For example, you are considering doing something but are not sure if you should. To know for sure, use the hierarchy of ideas to look at whether what you want to do is related to your vision and your purpose. For me, reading a book on Agile or change management is an exact match to my purpose. Watching five episodes of *Revenge* in a row … well, not exactly. It won't necessarily stop me from doing what I want to do, but it will give me an indication of how much time I should be dedicating to that activity. Just as you tightly manage the scope and range of activities on your project, you can be just as careful with your own time. Spending time on activities directly related to your own vision and purpose can be energising and exciting. Spending time on activities not related can be deflating.

Changing Your Vision

Having a vision and a purpose is critical. Sticking to these no matter what can have great benefits. And as we talked about before, they can give deep insight into how we are spending our time. However, revising our vision can be beneficial too. The world is changing faster than ever and sometimes the thing we set out to do is either not as appealing or no longer relevant.

The law of requisite variety (or the first law of cybernetics) states:

> *In any system, the element or person in the system with the widest range of behaviours or variability of choice will control the system.*

What does this mean? It means that the more behaviourally flexible you are, the more control you have over your life. So being flexible and willing to adapt is not just necessary in order to be excellent, it's critical to surviving in this fast-paced world.

BEING FLEXIBLE IS ESSENTIAL...

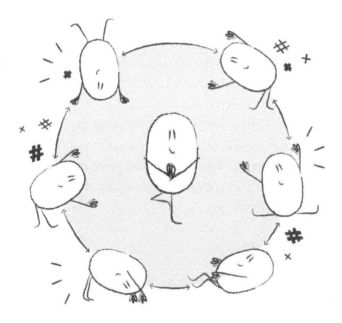

So if your purpose is not working for you, sit down and think about it again. What do you truly want? And what will that give you? What really gives you a fire in your belly? Go back to the five questions in Chapter 2. You may need to ask them again. And you may get different answers.

Self-Management in Times of Crisis

No matter how amazing our vision is and how committed we are to achieving it, stuff happens that can put our bodies and minds into a state of stress that is hard to manage. Our bodies are naturally attuned to respond to potential threats to our survival by either staying and fighting or running away (the well-known 'fight or flight' response). There is another response that involves freezing on the spot and doing nothing, and Adam Fraser describes this very well in his book *The Third Space*. All three responses are natural and were helpful back in the time when our everyday survival was threatened by predators or potential starvation.

Fortunately, these threats no longer exist, but the possibility of being fired, an angry sponsor looking for urgent answers or a difficult stakeholder disrupting your steering committee all induce these primal responses anyway. Whether it is fear of starvation or fear of a hungry predator, we can't help but respond in this way without thinking. This usually leads to less than optimal outcomes. The successful Agile PM chooses to respond to these challenges in a resourceful way, because simply reacting without thinking is a bad idea and almost always ends in disaster.

Much has been written on how to control the 'pause between stimulus and response', including in my coaching blog. Your ability to do this well will ultimately lead to a successful outcome in a threatening situation. But in the moment, this is not as easy as it sounds. In fact, it is sometimes so hard that the instant when you could have chosen the resourceful response has come and gone before you realised it was even there.

You can practise this pause and get better over time, which I highly recommend. Knowing your purpose helps in these situations. Really knowing your purpose. Because when you know it and you believe in it, you act consistently with that purpose every time. This includes the time when your project or personal success is threatened by a 'predator'. Knowing how to respond in that pause is as natural as any past reactions you may have had that did not lead to a positive outcome. The cool thing is, the better you become at responding to crises resourcefully, the more sure you become of your purpose. It may even adjust and become clearer, because whether we like it or not, our very best often comes out when crises hit.

The key to staying true to your vision is self-management in times of crisis. The key to self-management in times of crisis is HAVING a vision in the first place. You see what I did there?

Time to Review Your Vision

In Chapter 1, we talked about the importance of having a vision and how to create one. Now, with the remainder of the toolkit that you need in order to be a successful Agile PM, has that vision changed? Does it need reviewing? Is it big enough? Is it something you can grow into?

Because even in the course of a project, while it is important to stay true to the project vision and purpose, sometimes that vision needs to change due to external forces such as the market, competition or drastic economic change.

This is why it is important to have a project and personal vision that is so compelling that it lights up the room. It will tap into something bigger than you and keep you on track to achieve success.

Key Learning Points

- Stay true to your vision but be flexible

- Have strategies ready to cope with crisis

- Check in on your vision often – is it still relevant?

CONCLUSION

There's a lot to consider when aiming for excellence as an Agile PM. And before it gets overwhelming, remember one of the most important Agile practices: observation of the Pareto principle or 80/20 rule. The Pareto principle broadly states that, for many events, approximately 80% of the effects come from 20% of the causes. It was suggested by management consultant Joseph M. Juran that it be named after Vilifredo Pareto, who first published a paper in 1896 observing that 80% of the land in Italy was owned by 20% of the population. Apparently he also observed that 20% of the pea pods in his garden contained 80% of the peas (unverified). Many studies have proven to varying degrees that 20% of effort yields 80% of results. This is very exciting for the Agile PM, who aims to get the most value as early as possible in their projects.

When it comes to learning and applying new things, the great Agile PM will take away what is most valuable and apply it immediately, rather than trying to change too much too soon. So when you think about the changes you are working through now – both professional and personal – which practices and principles would help you the most right now?

Focus on where you can obtain the most value, as increased effort (using time you simply do not have) has diminishing returns.

> "Perfect is the enemy of good."
>
> Voltaire

Key Learning Points

Vision – both for your project and for yourself – is the cornerstone of being a great Agile PM. When you know where you are going, how you get there works itself out. Not sure of your project vision? Start by asking why, and for what purpose are we doing what we are doing. Chunk up to a level where the key stakeholders understand and agree. Not sure if you should be doing what you are doing right now? Again, ask why. Does this link to your purpose? How important is this? Be open and flexible to change, because you never know what amazing opportunities are just around the corner.

Risks – know them, plan for them and do everything you can to make life easy for yourself. Consider different people's styles when anticipating risk and use these to your advantage to ensure all bases are covered. Remember, people are always looking for what is in it for them and any potential risk could be perceived as being a personal threat to their very survival. Be okay with role playing potential scenarios and anticipating consequences for certain decisions. This not only anticipates problems before they start, but in the process helps stakeholders feel safe.

People – know your team and who you can count on, both inside and outside your project. Everyone is different and has unique value to add. Consider their ways of taking in information to ensure you keep them engaged and excited about what you are doing. The power of an inspired team working toward a clear vision together is a force to be reckoned with, especially when the team members feel safe and that they are playing to their strengths.

Scope – align what you are doing with why you are doing it. A great vision identifies your Musts and ensures you are only doing what is aligned to your vision. It simplifies everything and allows a great Agile PM to set boundaries both on the professional and personal front. Being clear about who you are and what you stand for makes it easy to make those day-to-day decisions about what really must be done, and what can be done later or not at all.

Systems, tools and processes – sustain yourself over time with great habits and practices. Keep them simple and easy to support you over time. Know when you are at your best, so you always give your best. So when you're not at your best, you can turn to tried and true practices to get you through times of uncertainty.

Opportunities for excellence – always be on the lookout to become even more excellent than you already are. Not to be confused with 'gold plating', opportunities for excellence show you are always thinking outside the box so you are delivering not just what is expected but the very most value possible. Cultivate a mindset of excellence so you don't just deliver projects, you deliver them so well that you always get the best feedback and the best gigs.

Consider this your personal checklist for change.

Teach Someone Else

Have you learned something valuable from this book that you want to remember and take into your day-to-day life? Remember, the best way to ensure that you never forget something is teaching it to someone else (remember lens 3 from Chapter 1?) Who could you share with the valuable thing you have learned that could make a difference for them?

What are the three key learnings from the book you could pass on to someone else?

1. _____

2. _____

3. _____

Your Personal Action Plan

If this book was the best book you have ever read, with the most profound impact on your life, why would this be the case? What are three key actions you can take away right now and apply immediately? Write them down here:

1. _____

2. _____

3. _____

Take Action

"We all know that nothing moves until something moves."

Albert Einstein

Often we wait for a feeling or something outside ourselves to happen. Sometimes it does and we take action as a result. But a lot of the time, it doesn't. This means we have to take action BEFORE we feel like it. We need our physiology to take control of our psychology.

Amy Cuddy's inspiring presentation in 2012 at TED Global on what she calls "power poses" is among the most viewed TED Talks of all time (it is actually number 2 – Sir Ken Robinson's *How Schools Kill Creativity* is No. 1). Her research studied people who were told they were going to be interviewed. Half the study group were asked to sit hunched over for a period of time before their interview. Others were told to stand up with their arms in the air and big smiles on their faces. During their interviews, others observed them and rated whether they thought they would get the job. These people had no knowledge of what the interviewees had been doing before the interview. Most observers favoured the people who had been standing in "power poses" before their interview. If this wasn't amazing enough, the interviewees' saliva was tested following their poses and the ones who had been standing up in the "power pose" were found to have higher levels of testosterone and lower levels of the stress hormone cortisol than the interviewees who had been hunched over.

This is a great one to test. Hunch over and look down for thirty seconds. How do you feel? Now stand up, look up and throw your arms in the air. Stay there for a few seconds. How do you feel now? Different, right?

Taking action can change everything, so take action today. And let me know how you go. I love hearing from fellow Agile PMs who are putting these concepts into practice. I believe that if enough people embrace these principles and concepts, and take action, we will see an evolution of project management beyond anything we have experienced so far.

The world is changing. And the way we manage change will continue to change. The principles and ideas in this book give us the opportunity to evolve beyond the traditional confines of industrially inspired project management. By focusing on what is really important and striving for excellence, we will not only survive but also thrive, achieving our purpose and aspirations, so that change happens on our terms. We just need to be ready.

Are you ready?

GLOSSARY OF TERMS

Burn-up chart

A visual map of how the project is progressing. It is visible at all times on the team wall.

This chart allows a sponsor, PM, team and stakeholders to understand the progress of the project, so they can make timely and informed decisions throughout the project.

Epic

Sometimes called a large user story that is too high level to be worked on but needs to be broken into smaller chunks – or user stories.

Estimation sessions

A meeting organised within the project team with representatives from everyone taking part in the work. The team works together to apply relative weightings to each user story to represent the effort required to deliver the functionality in the user story. Differences in estimations are discussed and agreement reached. Sometimes called planning poker.

Extreme Programming (XP)

A type of Agile software development designed to improve software quality and responsiveness to changing customer requirements. It advocates releasing output in short development cycles with checkpoints as opportunities to adopt any new customer requirements

Iteration/Sprint

A pre-agreed set time (between 2 and 4 weeks) when a pre-agreed list of user stories is developed, tested and showcased to stakeholders. Like a mini-project cycle.

Iteration Manager/ Scrum Master

A person who manages the day-to-day activities of the project team. As the team is mostly self-managing, this role guides the team and ensures good Agile practices are being followed, team members feel supported and the visual management is kept up to date. They also remove impediments so the team can run effectively and will escalate where required to resolve issues and blockers. The term 'iteration manager' comes from XP (Extreme Programming) and 'Scrum master' comes from Scrum and are often used interchangeably, but these roles are slightly different in that the iteration manager is responsible for the team's deliverables, while in Scrum, the team takes full responsibility for its deliverables. This is a subtle difference and often overlooked.

Jira

System used to track user stories and their progress at a more detailed level than a project wall.

Kanban/Lean

Kanban is Japanese for 'visual signal' or 'card'. The concept is used extensively in manufacturing and was inspired by W. Edwards Deming. Often project walls are called 'Kanban walls' as they visually represent the flow of work being done.

This also standardises cues and refines processes, which helps to reduce waste and maximise value for a project team.

Principles (source: www.Agilemanifesto.org)

Formalised by a group of software development experts in 2001:

- Our highest priority is to satisfy the customer through early and continuous delivery of valuable software.

- Welcome changing requirements, even late in development. Agile processes harness change for the customer's competitive advantage.

- Deliver working software frequently, from a couple of weeks to a couple of months, with a preference for the shorter timescale.

- Business people and developers must work together daily throughout the project.

- Build projects around motivated individuals. Give them the environment and support they need, and trust them to get the job done.

- The most efficient and effective method of conveying information to and within a development team is face-to-face conversation.

- Working software is the primary measure of progress. Agile processes promote sustainable development. The sponsors, developers and users should be able to maintain a constant pace indefinitely.

- Continuous attention to technical excellence and good design enhances agility.

- Simplicity – the art of maximising the amount of work not done – is essential.

- The best architectures, requirements and designs emerge from self-organising teams.

- At regular intervals, the team reflects on how to become more effective, then tunes and adjusts its behaviour accordingly.

Product Backlog

Estimated, prioritised collection of work items (represented by user stories). The backlog evolves regularly (often referred to as 'backlog grooming') to ensure priorities are always represented and any changes are reflected.

Product Owner

Someone (usually someone from the business) who is accountable for:

- setting direction and priorities

- representing the commercial aspects of the project (i.e. benefits realisation)

- ensuring the product backlog is up-to-date and prioritised according to business value

- ensuring all business stakeholders are represented.

Retrospective

Session organised after every iteration/sprint or release to provide the team and sometimes stakeholders with the opportunity to share what they felt went well, did not go well and could do better in the following sprints. Every retrospective ends with actions and timeframes assigned, with the team and stakeholders agreeing on what to focus on to improve.

Scrum

A framework that means iterative development, mainly applied to software. It is the most widely recognised term and what most organisations adopt, at least in part. It is from Scrum that the terms 'sprint' or 'iteration' come and it also uses daily stand-ups, retrospectives and showcases. Sometimes Scrum is used interchangeably with Agile. This is not correct: Scrum is a specific framework under the Agile umbrella.

Shippable product

A term often heard in the development of software that refers to an outcome that is ready for release to the customer. The focus in Agile is in completing shippable products as much as possible, no matter how small.

Showcase

A session used to demo the working functionality delivered during the last iteration/sprint and present the latest burn-up chart. The sponsor and any other interested stakeholders are usually in attendance and direction is adjusted if needed. This is an information and decision-making forum.

Spike

A task or story aimed at gathering information prior to an actual story being written and developed. Ideally a spike to find information or answer a question will happen in the sprint prior to this information being required. A spike does not directly contribute to a shippable product, but is still estimated and taken into account.

Stand-ups

Short (usually 15-minute) daily get together where all members from the project team stand around the physical storyboard/wall displaying the user stories and tasks that are being worked on. Everyone gives a brief update on: what they did yesterday, what they will be doing today, any issues or blockers and what help they need if there are issues/blockers.

Story Wall/Board

A visual display of user stories/task cards which shows project progress. You should be able to easily see what cards are in the backlog, what are in progress and what have been completed.

Super showcase

Similar to a showcase, but a super showcase can demo the working functionality delivered over a number of iterations to present a bigger picture of what has been delivered. Usually done at the end of a release.

Task

In Scrum, user stories are broken into tasks that can be completed within a day or two. The team works together to break stories down and ensures tasks are allocated to each other based on availability and experience. The idea is that the tasks flow easily across the storyboard to show continuous progress.

User Story

Similar to a requirement. A story is a piece of work that describes the work that needs to be done. Every story will have a clear outcome as well as a definition of 'done' – the universal term that defines the work being complete.

Values (source: www.Agilemanifesto.org)

Formalised by a group of software development experts in 2001:

- Individuals and interactions over processes and tools

- Working software over comprehensive documentation

- Customer collaboration over contract negotiation

- Responding to change over following a plan

Velocity

The rate at which work is completed. Critical in measuring the team's capacity so future planning can be accurate. Generally, velocity starts off slowly as the team starts working together, especially if they are new to working with Agile, but it is expected to increase. Generally, the average of the first three iterations is a good prediction of future velocity.

Waterfall

The traditional method for developing and implementing software. It breaks down the project into distinct phases where all of the requirements are gathered first, then there is a complete design phase, followed by testing and implementation. The key issue with this approach is that there is no flexibility to change and no opportunity to check in regularly. It also means that all value is delivered at the end, as opposed to opportunities to deliver value along the way.

Keep up to date on new terms by visiting here: http://theagileprojectmanager.com.au/glossary/

INSPIRATION AND REFERENCES

They say there is no such thing as a brand new idea. I think there are a lot of great new ideas out there that have both been discovered and are yet to be discovered. And those new ideas need help in the form of inspiration from other ideas. In creating this book I drew upon inspiration from so many people, places and movements that I would love to acknowledge them. These sources include:

The Manifesto for Agile Software Development: www.manifesto.org

A Guide to the Project Management Body of Knowledge (PMBOK Guide) – Fifth Edition, Project Management Institute (PMI).

ETM Management Solutions: www.etmmanagement.com.au

Simon Sinek's TED Talk: How Great Leaders Inspire Action: www.ted.com/talks/simon_sinek_how_great_leaders_inspire_action

Simon Sinek: *Start with Why* (2011, www.startwithwhy.com). An inspirational book and entire movement. I listened to the audio book, which was brilliant as he narrates beautifully.

Margie Warrell: *Stop Playing Safe* (2013) and *Brave* (2015). Wonderful books on courage and living your dreams.

Albert Bandura: *Self Efficacy: The Exercise of Control* (1997).

Tali Sharot's TED Talk (2012): The Optimism Bias: www.ted.com/talks/tali_sharot_the_optimism_bias?language= en#t-36167

Rob Thomsett: *Third Wave Project Management: A Handbook for managing the Complex Information Systems for the 1990s* (1993), *Radical Project Management (2002)* and *The Agile Project Manager's Toolkit* (2009).

Tony Robbins: *Unlimited Power – the new science of personal achievement* (1997).

Richard Beckhard & Wendy Pritchard: *Changing the Essence: The Art of Creating and Leading Fundamental Change in Organizations* (1992).

Everett Rogers: *Diffusion of Innovations* (1967).

Simon T. Bailey: *Shift your Brilliance* (2014, www.simontbailey.com). I read the entire book nodding my head excitedly in complete agreement over his thoughts on how much of an impact our environment can have on our results.

Mark Denne & Jane Cleland-Huang: *Software by Numbers: Low-Risk, High-Return Development* (2004).

Kurt Lewin: *The Turning Point: Science, Society, and the Rising Culture* (1943).

Peter Taylor: *The Lazy Project Manager* (2010, www.thelazyprojectmanager.com). I read Peter's book a number of years ago and admired his ability to describe project management in terms that were not only simple but fun. After reading it, I promised myself I would do something like that one day.

Dr Jason Fox: *The Game Changer* (2014). A great book with a surprising twist on the concept of motivation.

Stephen Covey: *The Seven Habits of Highly Effective People* (2004).

Daniel Goleman: *Emotional Intelligence: Why it can matter more than IQ* (1995).

Dr Adam Fraser: *The Third Space* (2012).

Amy Cuddy's TED Talk (2012): Your body language shapes who you are: www.ted.com/talks/amy_cuddy_your_body_language_shapes_who_you_are

Malcolm Gladwell: *Blink* (2007) and *Outliers* (2011). Well worth the audio books, as they are both beautifully narrated by the author.

Brene Brown: *Daring Greatly* (2015). Another amazing woman encouraging others to get "into the arena" and not hold back from achieving greatness.

Robin Sharma: *The Leader who had no Title* (2010, www.robinsharma.com) – a great reminder we can all be a leader in everything we do without the formal title, but just being who we are. This is particularly true for Agile teams, which have a flat structure and social norms that encourage members to call each other out for non-team like behaviours.

Deepak Chopra: all of his work is so uplifting and inspiring, and a reminder of what is important in life.

Dr Wayne Dyer: I have read almost all his books and was fortunate to go to his seminar in Melbourne a short week before he passed away. He inspired me in so many ways, the main way being to remind me that I have more control over my results than I realise. A special thanks to Hay House for giving me permission to quote his work.

Next steps

To order a copy of this book, please go to

www.theagileprojectmanager.com.au

Would you like to work with me?

I run workshops and trainings on all these concepts as well as one-on-one and group coaching.

I am also available to speak at your next event.

Get in touch via the website or +61 404 624 314.

Connect with me

Twitter: @emmawhitecat

Facebook: www.facebook.com/theagileprojectmanager

LinkedIn: https://au.linkedin.com/in/emmabrycesharrock